GEORGE LAYCOCK

Strange
Monsters
AND GREAT SEARCHES

DOUBLEDAY & COMPANY, INC., GARDEN CITY, NEW YORK

By George Laycock

THE ALIEN ANIMALS

ANIMAL MOVERS

THE DEER HUNTER'S BIBLE

THE DILIGENT DESTROYERS

THE PELICANS

THE SHOTGUNNER'S BIBLE

THE SIGN OF THE FLYING GOOSE

WILD REFUGE

STRANGE MONSTERS AND GREAT SEARCHES

ISBN: 0-385-03463-6 Trade
       0-385-03818-6 Prebound
Library of Congress Catalog Card Number 72-76185
Copyright © 1973 by George Laycock
All Rights Reserved
Printed in the United States of America

CONTENTS

1

THE MYSTERY OF LOCH NESS

THERE LIVES, some say, a gigantic monster, in a beautiful lake in the Highlands of Scotland. It has come to the surface just often enough to puzzle and frighten people of the region and keep them speculating about the identity of their monster. By now more than one thousand people claim to have seen the mysterious serpent believed to dwell in the depths of Loch Ness.

Loch Ness is a beautiful place for a monster to live. The lake, long, narrow, and deep, is flanked by high green hills where dew and fog and frequent rains keep the blankets of lush vegetation dripping with moisture. Clouds pile up in the valleys. From the high vantage points travelers sometimes look down, not only on the loch, but on the clouds as well. The centuries have not robbed this magic scene of its sense of loneliness and quiet. Beside the lake stand ancient abandoned castles. Nearby is an age-old monastery, and people living around the lake occupy the lands their ancestors held.

For twenty-three miles Loch Ness stretches along its valley. It connects with the sea through the River Ness. Within the river a system of navigation locks permits passage of boats from salt water into fresh, and some say provides opportunity as well for a traveling sea serpent to slip in and out as the mood strikes. It would, of course, not be the only creature to live part of its life in salt water and the rest in fresh. Fish known to move from salt water into fresh-water streams for spawning are classified as anadromous. The lake is scarcely more than a mile wide through most of its length but goes down to a depth of 754 feet.

These waters are stained dark brown from draining through beds of peat en route to the lake. One can not peer more than a few feet into the dim hidden world beneath the surface. Therefore observers must depend on this serpent to come to the surface, or out on land, if they are ever to see it.

Many do not believe. The Loch Ness monster, they sometimes hint, is not in there at all. This, in fact, is what William Brodie, captain of a steam tug operating on the lake, used to think. "Humbug," said Captain Brodie, "Loch Ness monster indeed!"

Then one summer afternoon in 1938, when his tug was pushing along steadily across the fog-shrouded lake, there appeared out of the depths a creature unknown to all on board. For a short distance it swam along beside the tug boat. It was long and slender, and humps on its back stuck out of the water as the humps of a sea serpent are supposed to do.

Next the creature turned on the power, spurted ahead of the boat, and finally dived. A short time later it appeared again far out in front, still increasing its lead on the sluggish boat where Captain Brodie stood wide-eyed on the bridge.

The captain had joined the believers. "There can," he is quoted as saying, "be no doubt of the monster's existence."

Others who have been startled by sight of the creature hasten to agree. For example, there was a motorcyclist named Grant who, some years ago, was speeding along the north shore road beside Loch Ness in the darkness of night. Suddenly, in the beam of his headlight there emerged from the woods a creature such as he had never before witnessed. Nobody wants to go crashing willy-nilly into a monster, and Mr. Grant maneuvered skillfully to avoid the collision.

Just why a sea serpent should cross the road is one of the big mysteries. To explain it away simply by saying that it ". . . wants to get on the other side," seems hardly adequate. But the Loch Ness monster has been reported on other occasions too, as coming out of the water to make its way overland for short distances. Mr. Grant reported that as he caught the form of the creature in the light of his cycle, it made two bounds and cleared the road, then quickly sloshed back into Loch Ness, there to vanish beneath the foaming surface. It was, he estimated, between fifteen and twenty feet long, had a small head, beady eyes, long slender neck, and appeared to be dark and slimy.

Another report of the Loch Ness monster being out of its water came from John McKay. Mr. McKay operated a hotel nearby and one spring evening in 1933 was out driving with his wife over the newly completed road along the north shore of the lake. There in plain sight was "Nessie" as folks around Loch Ness have come to know their sea serpent. The creature at once dived into the lake.

Later Mr. McKay reported to a local newspaper what he and his wife had seen. The story spread rapidly. The Loch Ness monster became world famous in the years that followed. Books have since been written about it. Countless newspaper accounts have told of its appearances. Expeditions have been mounted to unravel the mystery. Meanwhile around Loch Ness, and throughout Scotland, people have divided into three camps. There are those who believe, those who doubt, and those who keep an open mind.

Nessie has been around a long time. For hundreds of years there have been stories around Loch Ness of the monster that roams the depths of the lake. It was written centuries ago that a "certain water monster" was driven away by prayer. But the effects of the prayer apparently were temporary.

Over the years legends about the sea serpent were passed down from generation to generation. It is said in one such legend to have killed a man. Folks around the loch have long felt that the creature might reappear at any moment.

But not until reported again by Mr. McKay in 1933 did

Nessie rise to true prominence. As the story spread, more people began watching for the monster. People who want to see a monster stand a far better chance than those who do not care one way or the other. This is more in the nature of people than monsters.

Perhaps no monster has ever done more for people anywhere than has the Loch Ness monster. Living or dead, real or not, it has to be the most valuable creature ever possessed by the Scottish people. Those who have come seeking it have brought a new source of wealth to the country.

As the stories of Nessie spread around the world the people of Scotland began to notice a strange and wonderful result. Curious tourists now planned their travels to include the Highlands of Scotland and Loch Ness, home of the world's best-known sea serpent. From all parts of the world they come now to the town of Inverness.

Many of them board the *Scott II* and travel out onto the lake, sharing for a few hours the mystery-shrouded environment of the serpent's ancient home. The *Scott II* makes three trips daily. From Inverness it goes to about the middle of the lake, turns, and comes back to its dock. Lining its rails are the curious ones.

Many insist that they do not believe the tales of the sea serpent, that they come only because they have for so long wanted to see the Highlands and hear the strains of the bagpipes moaning with the winds.

But instead of looking up to the hills, their eyes more often are turned down upon the dark waters of Loch Ness. Cameras hang from their necks. Binoculars are ready in their hands. These are the ones who do not know quite what to believe. What did John McKay really see? What was this strange unnatural creature sighted by Captain Brodie and so many others? How could it have been seen so many times and not be there? Surely there is the possibility that all the people living around the lake, the ones who insist, "There has to be something out there," may be right. And so the visitors hopefully study the rippling waters of Loch Ness.

Some outsiders have devised elaborate plans for capturing or killing the beast and transporting it to a museum, zoo, or circus. A giant electronic net has been suggested, and so has the possibility of shooting it from a submarine. In efforts to prevent monster poaching, officials have passed regulations, perhaps the only rules in the world against the harming of a sea serpent.

Most who come to study the mystery of Scotland's sea serpent, however, have no plans to harm it. They seek only truth, the opportunity to solve for good the centuries-old mystery.

Some come in groups with camping equipment. Above the loch they set up their tents and post serpent watchers. Some have made pictures of strange forms appearing on the lake. One of the most famous pictures shows a long slender neck, small head, part of the tail, all attached to a large balloon-like body.

Perhaps no one has studied the Loch Ness monster more than Tim Dinsdale has. For long days and weeks he wandered the shores of Loch Ness. He carried cameras and binoculars and possessed a grim determination to prove that the monster does exist. His hunt for the creature is outlined in his two books on the subject. He has little patience with the non-believers, especially the men of science who steadfastly refuse to join the search for the serpent of Loch Ness. Dinsdale says they simply ignore the facts.

The case for a sea serpent in Loch Ness is strengthened, according to fans of Nessie, by the appearance of similar creatures in other parts of the world. For example, there is the monster of Lake Okanagan, British Columbia, in western Canada. This lake, in some ways resembles Loch Ness, long, narrow, and almost as deep, with cold water and a good population of fish. There have also been frequent reports of a monstrous serpent living in a lake in Manitoba in central Canada.

Perhaps if science would apply its efforts to the search for the Loch Ness monster the mystery might be solved. So far most of the work has been done, not by scientists, but by amateur monster hunters. Most of the serious work has been co-ordinated by the Loch Ness Phenomena Investigation Bureau Ltd.

More than once there has been the suggestion that sonar is the tool for finding Nessie. Sonar is a method of using electronics to study what lies beneath the surface of water. It was developed during World War II for tracking submarines. Electric impulses are sent into the water. Converted to sound waves, they travel through the water spreading out into a broad cone as they leave the source.

When one of these waves strikes any obstacle under water, the impulse bounces back like an echo to be measured by the instrument that sent it. The length of time taken for it to return tells the depth of the object. The bottom of the lake will reflect the sound but so will obstacles appearing between the surface and the lake bottom. In addition, the sonar reveals the depth, size, and movement of whatever is down there.

In 1968 a scientific party moved in on Nessie with electronic locators. In due time the results were published in the *New Scientist,* a respected British scientific journal.

Engineers in a research team from the University of Birmingham set up their equipment on the shore of Loch Ness. Then, as the impulses traveled through the cold depths of Loch Ness, engineer D. Gordon Tucker carefully studied the screen of the sonar outfit.

Flickering signals began to echo to the machine. Together they told Tucker a fascinating story and opened a new possibility. There was, as the folks around Loch Ness had long insisted, something down there, and plainly it was not a wee monster. For 13 minutes two large objects had their images reflected as the signals were photographed on movie film. One was about 164 feet long, the other, somewhat smaller.

Did the image of these monsters move on the screen? Definitely! Their speed was about 17 miles an hour, and they dived at a rate of 450 feet per minute.

After these observations the research team quickly consulted with biologists who know the common fish of Loch Ness. Could a school of fish have caused this kind of signal? The answer was "not likely," and this to many observers was new evidence that Nessie might after all be real.

But if the Loch Ness monster does live, what in the world could it be? Investigators over the years have advanced two favored explanations. Some say it is the larvae of a giant eel.

Others insist that Nessie must be one of an ancient group of reptiles known as Plesiosaurs. One thing wrong with this theory is that Plesiosaurs are believed to have become extinct seventy million years ago. Perhaps it is just as well that we do not yet know for certain whether or not Loch Ness has a real monster.

Those who claim Nessie belongs to the Plesiosaurs might point out that scientists have been surprised before when they found "extinct" creatures still surviving. The best known example is the Coelacanth.

2

UNBELIEVABLE FISH

ONE DECEMBER DAY in 1938 the captain and crew of a fishing trawler were hard at work off the southern coast of Africa. Day after day, this business was the same. Set out the nets. Pull in the nets. Sort the fish. Haul them back to town on the mainland, sell them, then get ready to go out again.

During his years of commercial fishing the captain had brought up into the African sunlight every species of fish he could think of. There had been little fish, big fish, dull-colored creatures, and others to rival the rainbow. The captain believed, in fact, that he had seen about everything there was to see from down there in the deepening shadows.

But on this December day there was a strange fish, out

of the past, crawling sluggishly on the bottom some 250 feet beneath the surface. It watched the sleek forms of other fish that swam by, and its large muscular jaws snapped open and shut on any of them that chanced too close.

If the antique creature, half crawling and half swimming about on the ocean floor, had been a little faster he might have evaded the net. The net, stretching out through the water, moved closer and closer until there was no longer any way to escape it, and the next thing the creature realized it was being rolled and tumbled along by a force too strong to fight. Smaller fish were now all around him, but he had forgotten his hunger.

When the netful of fish was dumped out, the crew looked over the catch. Hundreds of fish were wiggling and squirming there in one pile. Then a crewman spotted the strange large fish the net had scooped off the ocean floor.

The captain saw it, scratched his grizzled chin, and shook his head in bewilderment. Nobody in the crew could recall seeing anything to match this one. Steel blue in color, the monster fish had large scales, weighed 125 pounds, and was 5 feet long. The crew members soon found that the fish was still alive. If they put a hand too close to its gaping jaws, it grabbed for them with those snapping sharp teeth. It lived four more hours.

By then the captain had decided that he would take this strange creature to the museum when he reached port. Perhaps the curator, Miss Courtenay-Latimer, could tell him what manner of creature he had dredged from the bounty of the sea.

By the time the trawler docked the fish was three days dead. The smell was something a person simply had to adjust to. The fish was so far gone that the museum curator could save only its skin and skull.

Miss Courtenay-Latimer was puzzled. But one who would surely know was Professor J. L. B. Smith. Professor Smith was located at the Albany Museum twenty-five miles west in Grahamstown. Miss Courtenay-Latimer sent off a wire to Professor Smith. A few days later Miss Courtenay-Latimer led him to the refrigerator in which she had stored the puzzling remains.

The story of fish, as Professor Smith and others of his profession know, goes back through the geologic ages to the very beginning of vertebrate life. Some of the story has been read in the record of the rocks where science has found clues in the fossils. Ancient and extinct creatures, washed into muddy deltas and buried in swamps, have had their forms preserved. By studying the rocks, layer by layer, scientists have unraveled the mysteries. From present back into the past, deeper and deeper, the trails lead. Not long ago there were the mastodons and the saber-toothed tigers, giant sloths, and giant beaver. These were early representatives of the mammals.

Back beyond the mammals there were the ages during which birds evolved, and further still the times when reptiles, including the giant dinosaurs, ruled the earth.

Millions of years before that, however, no vertebrate animals at all yet lived on land. All life was in the sea, and fishes were evolving from lower creatures. One step in this rise of animals has long drawn the attention of scientists. This is the mystery of how creatures of the seas finally came out onto land to live. Which of the fish fathered the land dwellers? What manner of creature ventured from those ancient seas millions of years ago to wander among the giant ferns and primitive plants?

One of the scientists who had studied this giant step in the animal kingdom was Professor Smith. He knew what the fossils had told science. Especially he knew about a group of ancient fish that scientists called "Coelacanths."

Hundreds of fossils of Coelacanths had already been dug up, stored in museums, studied, and written about in the annals of science. Many scientists were agreed, as they still are, that this was the group that gave rise to the land creatures. From some pioneering branch of the Coelacanth's family had emerged individuals able to adapt to life on land. Maybe in those changing ages, ponds dried and individuals struggling to locate new waters managed short, then longer trips over land. This is speculation.

So complete were fossils of the Coelacanth that scientists in their laboratories managed to unravel much of the story of this fish of long ago. It had, even in those days, scales that overlapped like shingles, a perfectly good design still found on today's fish. It possessed, most interestingly of all perhaps, strange stumps connecting its fin to its body. These short stumps reminded scientists of beginning legs, and it was easy to see that the fins of these primitive fish must have been used for crawling around the floor of the seas.

When scientists discussed Coelacanths they spoke of them in the past tense. All evidence pointed toward a story that ended millions of years ago. Saber-toothed tigers were gone. Mammoths were gone. Dinosaurs were gone. Thousands of species had evolved, flourished, then passed on, extinct and largely forgotten. The Coelacanth, according to the records of the rocks, had lived two hundred million years before the dinosaurs. They had lived in many parts of the world from South America, Africa, Europe, and Greenland. But they had started on their downward trail at least one hundred million years ago. The youngest fossil remains of them were judged to be seventy million years old. No wonder scientists spoke of the Coelacanth as history. Any creature that has been gone for seventy million years is extinct indeed. The marvel of it was that scientists millions of years later knew almost exactly what the Coelacanth looked like when it was still crawling about the seas.

Meanwhile, back in the lab, Miss Courtenay-Latimer opened the refrigerator, removed the remains, and looked questioningly at the learned Professor Smith. Slowly there spread across his countenance a strange expression. He felt as if he had stepped into a time capsule and been whisked back through the history of the earth ten million years, twenty million, seventy million. Before him was the remains of a true Coelacanth. Only days before it had been alive, crawling about on the bottom of the sea.

Understandably, when word of this identification flashed out from South Africa to scientists around the world, many were stunned. Some frankly did not believe it. The Coelacanth was extinct. It had been extinct all those millions of years. And that was that. But the story was soon confirmed.

This set in motion one of the most heartbreaking searches in all the world of natural history. In the following weeks Professor Smith wanted, more than anything else in the world, to have another Coelacanth. He wanted one that was whole so specialists could study its organs and structure part by part. What facts such a specimen might reveal!

First, Professor Smith asked himself where in the world men might stand the best opportunity of finding more of these strange creatures. A scientist experienced in the study of fish can, by looking at the outside of a fish, tell something of the kind of world it inhabits. The Coelacanth was no exception. Those strong scales would be protection against rough rocky ledges. The creature was obviously a slow mover, not a speeding, streamlined fish. Therefore the Coelacanth probably did not capture its prey by out-maneuvering the fish it ate. Instead, Professor Smith surmised, it must lurk like a demon in the shadows of rocky crevices, waiting for prey to swim by.

On the other hand there was every reason to believe the Coelacanth would take a fisherman's baited hook. Why then, in a part of the world where fishermen worked the waters every day in their perpetual search for food, had people not caught these creatures? The Coelacanth must live in deep waters. Deep waters, rough rocky ledges, places where strong currents sweep food fish past those menacing jaws. That was not the kind of place where a trawl net could work, and it was not the kind of habitat found where the trawler had taken the strange fish.

This set Professor Smith to thinking about the whole east coast of Africa. Where, along that stretch of land, were the reefs and deep waters that might harbor more Coelacanths? He had the advantage of knowing this section of the world thoroughly from his own studies. Northward toward the Equator, along the shore of Madagascar, around such island groups as the Comores, those were the places to concentrate in the search.

Next the professor wrote a circular showing a drawing of the Coelacanth and offering a reward of one hundred pounds (about eight hundred dollars) to anyone who could bring him one. "Look carefully at this fish," the circular told thousands of fishermen along the coast and through the islands, "it may bring you good fortune. If you have the good fortune to catch or find one, do not cut or clean it any way but get it whole at once to a cold storage."

Hopefully thousands of these circulars were distributed along the coast. The months dragged into years. Professor Smith never gave up. Somewhere there had to be more Coelacanths. His search continued.

Fourteen years passed. Ahmed Hussein had been fishing, as he often did, with hook and line about two hundred yards off the shore. He struggled to bring a tremendous fish into his boat. Next day he took it to town to the market place and offered it for sale, hoping someone wanted a fish so large and fat.

But one of his friends in the market showed him a wrinkled scrap of paper, a copy of Professor Smith's circular. Together they studied the picture. Hussein became more and more excited.

Some days later, in a special airplane supplied by the government, Professor Smith arrived. There on the deck of a friend's ship was a box with the contents packed in soft materials.

The professor was too nervous to unwrap the fish, and the crew laid back the covering. By then the professor was on his knees beside the box. He took one quick look at the magnificent antique fish. The long search was ended. "I'm not ashamed," the professor later wrote, "to say that I wept. It was a Coelacanth."

During the next few years others were found, and scientists in their laboratories studied these links with a lost age.

What they learned only strengthened their earlier conclusions. This was not, as some said, the exact creature that had adapted to walk on land and led to reptiles, birds, and all other land vertebrates, including man, but it was of the same family.

There had been many kinds of Coelacanths. They had been much alike wherever they lived throughout the world. Even these that had survived into the twentieth century were scarcely changed from those ancient fossil forms. A member of this family had bridged the gap between the animals of land and sea.

In the world of science, the Coelacanth has been hailed as the greatest biological discovery of the century.

3

OLD MOSE

EARLY IN THIS CENTURY the high mountain country of south-central Colorado was home to a monster with a reputation that sent chills up the spines of strong men. If word went out that "Old Mose" had been sighted, ranch wives kept their small children indoors, and men were seen to inspect their rifles with special care. All of them knew they were dealing with the biggest grizzly bear ever known in those mountains. They also knew this bear had tasted human flesh.

Under the best conditions men and grizzly bears have never been very good neighbors. This feud between man and these giant North American bears began when explorers first invaded the bear's habitat. Lewis and Clark, exploring up the Missouri Valley, met the grizzly and were amazed. Then the famous mountain men, Jim Bridger, and all the rest, had the grizzly bears for neighbors. Neighborhood relationships never did warm up between the two species. Men despised the grizzlies for killing calves, sheep, and colts, and for threatening people. But they hated the grizzly most for another reason; the giant bears were hard to kill. Sometimes a man would have to shoot a grizzly half a dozen times. Any bear that didn't know when to lie down and die was not to be trusted.

These biggest of the bears, known for their humped backs and dish-shaped faces, once roamed over most of the western half of the United States. Rifles, traps, and poison took care of that. In the United States today, the grizzly bears are in Yellowstone and Glacier national parks, and even there they stay far back in the wilderness minding their own business most of the time. But, even though they are gone from ranch country almost everywhere, stories of them are still repeated.

Right in the heart of Old Mose's former range lay the Stirrup Ranch. This spread was then owned by Wharton H. Pigg who raised cattle and horses. Mr. Pigg was first aware that the giant bear's territory overlapped with his own one day in 1882 when he came upon the bear's trail. He reined his horse to a halt to gaze at the tracks in amazement. Along this trail had walked a bear with feet bigger than dish pans and on one of them a toe was missing.

Then other ranchers and hunters began to sight the monstrous grizzly elsewhere along the mountain range. All agreed that this must be a bear larger than they had ever seen, a frightening monster. This bear obviously deserved a name, and someone called him "Old Mose."

Indications are that Old Mose might have been young in those days. He lived on for enough years to cause more trouble than anyone really needed. He became a champion at robbing corrals. By the size of his foot and that missing toe ranchers were always able to tell when the giant grizzly had paid a visit.

As long as Old Mose lived, Mr. Pigg pursued him. He learned to understand the bear's habits. It seems likely that Old Mose also learned to understand the schemes dreamed up by Mr. Pigg. At any rate, over the years, they periodically tracked each other. Each, perhaps, was aware that a close confrontation would bring both into mortal danger.

As the years rolled by, the bear's transgressions increased. He had a fondness for fresh meat. Nobody knows how many head of stock he killed during his lifetime. The records reveal that he killed at least three full-grown bulls.

Killing a steer, or even a horse, was no big thing for Old Mose. A single swat with one of those powerful front feet would send the creature into the hereafter. A slashing bite in the neck would guarantee the job.

These crimes were truly bad in ranching country. But Old Mose soon earned an even more notorious reputation. The bear had been leading the good life in the vicinity of Black Mountain through the summer and into the fall of 1883. He was a loner, traveling wherever the urge took him. Sometimes he would turn up the sod, seeking tender roots of plants. Other times he would pause to harvest wild berries or snack on grubs. But a body that big needs considerable food, and whenever hunger grew strong enough, Old Mose turned his thoughts to food that came in large servings. Ranchers found the remains of several cows during those months.

Meanwhile the fame of Old Mose was spreading. There is a rule that guides the destinies of bounty hunters who pursue lawbreakers. The more famous the outlaw, the braver seems the man who shoots him. More and more men now dreamed of bringing Old Mose down. So three men set forth one autumn day to seek Old Mose in the high country. One of them was Jake Ratcliff. Jake fancied himself to be one big bear hunter.

For several days they hunted for sign of the giant grizzly. They watched for restless cattle. They studied the remains of carcasses. They watched for giant foot-prints.

Then, late one afternoon, they found exactly what they were seeking. Old Mose had taken his meal from the carcass of a steer, still warm where it had fallen. And around the kill were the unmistakable prints of the mammoth bear. Various trails led from the spot and the three men split up to see if one of them could rout the grizzly. One of them did.

The trail followed by Jake Ratcliff led to a bear-sized hole in the side of the hill. Outside the hole was a mound of fresh earth to tell Jake that a bear had been here shortly before.

Jake noticed that he was shaking slightly. A strange

chill chased up his spine, and he made a conscious effort to control his nerves. Jake had heard no noise and as far as he knew the breeze had not carried scent of his presence to the bear's sensitive nose. Or perhaps the grizzly had slipped off through the woods unnoticed. This would have been a lucky break for Jake Ratcliff.

Instead, Jake, moving quietly, soon spotted the massive bear. Quickly, he raised his rifle to his shoulder, aimed and fired, and the bullet struck the huge body. But nothing happened. All the bullets Ratcliff fired failed to bring the monster to earth.

From deep in the massive throat of the grizzly there came a horrible roar and then Old Mose turned upon the man. He charged down upon Ratcliff at full speed. Heavy brush will scarcely slow an enraged bear. Where he wanted to go, the underbrush parted. It was as if a tank were rumbling through. Before Ratcliff could get his feet in motion the bear was breathing in his face.

Old Mose reached for Ratcliff and threw him into the air like a mouse tossed by a cat. Experienced outdoorsmen know that the best defense when attacked by a bear is to lie perfectly still, and hope the bear leaves. Ratcliff, still conscious, now lay motionless and silent. Old Mose began to move off.

Finally the mutilated hunter, thinking the bear had gone, lifted his head to inspect the scene. This was all the clue Old Mose needed. Filled with pain from the bullets he carried, he had stood off to one side watching and waiting, and now leaped in once more on the man who had hurt him.

When the other hunters arrived they found Ratcliff still breathing. But Old Mose had finished his job. Jake Ratcliff died before morning.

Now Old Mose had really done it! He was guilty of the unforgivable. Word flashed across Colorado. The state had a killer grizzly on its hands. Every time the story was repeated the bear grew bigger, his exploits more daring.

But the giant grizzly had many active years ahead of him. Men tried every trick they could think of to succeed where Jake Ratcliff had failed.

If they set a trap, Old Mose would study it. If the trap had somehow been sprung, he would consume the bait before wandering on. But if the trap were still set, he would walk around it, leaving it untouched.

Mr. Pigg had another idea. He had observed that Old Mose sometimes went to the lake where he splashed and played in the cold water. Mr. Pigg waited until about time for the old bear to make his rounds of the mountain again.

When Old Mose arrived at the shore of the lake, there hidden in the shallow water, was a giant steel trap. The water masked out the man odor. Old Mose was not thinking of a trap as he splashed into the lake. He had no experience to tell him there was danger in the water.

Then he felt the trap spring. The monstrous bear leaped back, and with his lightning-fast reflexes almost escaped the trap completely. But the giant steel jaws had clamped shut on two toes of his right foot.

At that moment the son of a local rancher slipped down

to the lake's edge and peered through the aspen. What he saw sent him flying back to find Mr. Pigg. "Old Mose is down there all right," he yelled as he came up to Mr. Pigg, "right down there in the water caught in that trap sure as anything."

All men within hearing reached for their guns. The rumble of horses' hoofs sounded like a charge of cavalry. At last they had Old Mose, the killer grizzly, had him right where they wanted him. That's what they thought. By the time they reached the lake the massive bear had pulled free of the trap, leaving behind a part of his foot.

Old Mose went right on killing livestock. Bears have to eat. If he found a fence between himself and a calf, he might tear down the fence. If he found a colt in a corral, his method was to knock the corral down.

Year after year, Mr. Pigg and other hunters went into the mountains to test their skill. Some say that after finishing off Jake Ratcliff Old Mose killed other men, maybe three or four of them. If a human body was found anywhere within the old bear's range, Old Mose got the credit.

One of the newspapers of the day quoted an old-time rancher. "The stockmen of this country were in fear of their lives on account of this big bear. There were two or three men that had gone to the hills to look for him. They never returned and their bodies were never recovered."

Finally J. W. Anthony set out to find Old Mose. Mr. Anthony, who had killed many bears in his lifetime, had a pack of hounds that did his trailing. One April day in

1904, he and Mr. Pigg set off together to seek Old Mose.
Anthony came upon the bear first. His dogs had surrounded the monster in an aspen grove.

Mr. Anthony's mind flashed back to other bears he had
hunted. All were small when compared with the giant
that now stood snarling and roaring before him.

Then the first bullet struck the bear. Old Mose wheeled
about and rushed down upon the hunter just as he had
years earlier upon the hapless Jake Ratcliff. When Old
Mose was only three feet away, Mr. Anthony fired again.
The shot hit the giant between the eyes. Old Mose suddenly fell and died.

All that Old Mose ever wanted was to go where he
chose, eat what he liked, and not be hassled. But he
belonged to a species for which there was no longer space
in the West. And besides, he had a special problem; he
was a monster.

Men arrived to drag the huge body back to Stirrup
Ranch. They figured the bear weighed half a ton. The
hide was nine feet four inches long and nine and a half
feet wide.

One scientist, who later studied the brain of Old
Mose, concluded that the size of his brain was not very
big considering the bulk of his body. But for more than
twenty years the giant bear had been a match for every
man who pursued him.

4

DRAGONS OF KOMODO

IN THE FAILING YELLOW LIGHT of early evening the little fishing boat rocked gently in the bay off the quiet and mysterious island. The two-man crew stared up at the forbidding mountains. Were the tales they had heard of this place true? They were torn between two emotions, a deep curiosity and desire to go ashore to explore, and an equally deep fear of what they might find there.

This island in Indonesia, northwest of Australia, is one of the green dots of land in the blue Flores Sea. Elsewhere such islands might be famous for grass-skirted girls and guitar music. But no one then lived on this island in the chain, the island of Komodo, and it was known as the home of a remarkable dragon.

Up those slopes, toward the ancient volcanic peak towering two thousand feet above the sea, stretched green carpets of vegetation. Tall lontar palms stood on the hillsides like umbrellas on their long, clean trunks. Steep-walled canyons were choked with jungle-thick brush. It must be in these tangles that the giant reptiles with their long forked tongues and glaring eyes raced about on short scaly legs, devouring other creatures.

Perhaps the pearl fishermen drifting offshore were hungry for wild foods to supplement their constant diet of fish. Maybe they thought this island might provide a good base for their fishing operations. But they must have wondered, too, if the old folk had given them the straight story or simply fed them a preposterous tall tale. There was only one way to be sure.

They dropped anchor, sloshed ashore, and began climbing. Soon they paused to rest. While they stood there, one of them reached out and silently touched the arm of his companion. He nodded toward the trail ahead. Together they stood speechless, staring at the frightening beast that had waddled from the underbrush and now blocked their path while its beady eyes were trained upon them.

There is no record of how long it took the exploring fishermen to return to their boat. But later fishermen did establish a small outpost on Komodo, the island of the dragons.

This island of Komodo is a strange and lonely place where few outsiders come. It is one of a little cluster of islands formed long ago by volcanic action, pushing steam and molten rock from the sea. The islands are known as the Lesser Sundas, and they lie like gems in the blue sea east of Java. Strong currents and tides rip down through the passages around these islands, and these rough seas have discouraged visitors.

Komodo was not a great distance, however, from the museum in the town known today as Bogor, on Java. There the museum director, Major P. A. Ouwens, first heard the strange accounts as pearl fishermen told what they had seen on Komodo. Major Ouwens must have questioned the stories. Such tales are not easily believable. The year was 1912, and surely if there were monstrous dragons on Komodo, or anywhere else on earth for that matter, men of science would know of them by now.

On occasion, the governor of that group of islands made his rounds on an inspection tour. Never had there been reason for him to stop long on Komodo. Then, Major Ouwens made his strange request.

Would the governor mind, the next time he stopped around Komodo on his inspections, going inland a bit and seeing about this dragon thing?

When the governor arrived, he found two pearl fishermen on the island. They told him of dragons inhabiting the interior of the island. The governor even saw the remains of one of these lizards. He carried the story back to Ouwens, and the museum director was now on the trail of a new scientific discovery.

Major Ouwens decided to send an expedition to Komodo. As he made preparations for his staff to depart, he hesitated to tell anyone the objective of the trip. One could not blame him. Who would want the neighbors saying with raised eyebrows, "Did you hear about the major? He's sending an expedition they say, to search for dragons. Strange man, the major."

But what the major found from this visit to Komodo was soon to be repeated around the world, especially among scientists. Crawling on those green slopes were the creatures the world came to know as the Komodo dragons. They were cousins of the dinosaurs. Somehow they had survived through the ages into the present. They were, by far, the largest lizard anywhere on earth. One skin brought to the major measured thirteen feet.

Later others went to search for the Komodo dragons, and found them living also on the nearby island of Rintja, and a portion of Flores. Together these bits of land are but a speck on the map of the world. This is hostile country for the careless or unfortunate. Living here are deadly green vipers, cobras, wild boar, and water buffalo, while sharks and poisonous sea serpents cruise the edge of the sea.

No doubt Major Ouwens, like most of us, had been exposed to his share of dragon pictures and stories. In fairy tales any self-respecting dragon must have piercing eyes, long scaly tail, long, low body, and he should be a bit of a flame thrower, breathing fire out of his nostrils or perhaps his ears.

The Komodo dragon fell short of this on one point. It did not breathe fire. Otherwise the first one viewed by Major Ouwens possessed all the features a dragon could ask. The lizard was fully ten feet long. Later some were recorded at lengths of twelve and thirteen feet.

The head of the Komodo lizard is broad and flat and

covered with scales which overlap to form a rugged armor. His whole body is armor plated in this way. The eyes are set well back on the sides of the head. This gives him a wide field of vision, making it difficult to sneak up on him.

Out of his mouth flicks a long forked tongue that vibrates and tests the breezes for odors of food. His mouth is blood red on the inside. It opens like a cavern as the beast tears into his food. The mouth is so wide that most of the head is jaws, and rows of sharp edged teeth line the jaws and curve backward, hooking into and holding the food securely.

Each foot is equipped with five long sharp claws. These are useful in digging in the earth and also in tearing meat into bits. The tail is long and heavy and the giant lizard can flick it quickly and use it as a crushing weapon. The body is like a great wrinkled leather bag, dark bluish black with flecks of a yellowish undercast around the neck and underside.

Young Komodo dragons hatch from eggs about the size of goose eggs. From this small container emerges about twenty-one inches of long, slender reptile. The young are more yellowish than their elders and at once are very active. Young Komodo lizards dash all about and can even climb trees. Half grown ones five and six feet long have been known to climb into trees and lie along the branches over-hanging the jungle trail.

Most of the Komodo dragon's days and nights, however, are spent either feeding or resting. At rest he may lie quietly beside a game trail. Or he may hide in the darkness of one of the burrows he digs in the hillsides.

Because reptiles are cold blooded, these creatures seek the warmth of the sun. Lying there in the open, they turn with the sun, basking and adjusting from time to time to keep themselves comfortable.

Their appetite is fearsome to consider. Their most common food is carrion. They search out the dead deer, goats, wild boars, and water buffalo, and tear them into chunks for immediate consumption. Fresh meat seems to hold less appeal for them than it does once it has begun to rot. Men who have traveled to Komodo to trap or photograph the dragon, usually begin by putting out a dead goat for bait. After the meat has been a few days in the hot sun, the lizards' flicking, forked tongues begin to pick up the strong odors.

Then they come out of the dense cover to the food. As they hold the carrion down with their broad strong feet, their mighty jaws rip the flesh apart. There is nothing dainty about the eating habits of the lizard. Into those gaping red mouths go flesh, bones, hair and anything else in the way. A large Komodo dragon can swallow the entire hind quarter of a deer or goat in a single bite. As long as the food lasts, they continue to store it away in their expanding cavernous bodies.

To watch these largest of all living lizards eat carries an observer back millions of years into the dim age when dinosaurs ruled the earth.

Will these monsters attack live animals? "Yes," say those who have studied them. "They will attack a beast as large as a pony." Dashing out of hiding from the shadows of the trees, the giant lizards grab and hang onto their victim. But large animals sometimes break away and later carry scars as evidence of their brush with death.

There are no records of a Komodo dragon having attacked a man unprovoked. The human who sees one coming can outrun it. He might even set a new track record. When a Komodo dragon is captured, it struggles and fights fiercely. It snaps and grabs at anything or anyone within reach. But a dragon can be forgiven for this.

Today there are still populations of these giant lizards crawling about on their native islands, primarily on Komodo. But their numbers have dwindled, and their future is threatened. There may be no more than a few hundred of them remaining. They are listed now on the official roster of the world's rare and endangered wildlife. With them on the same list are nearly one thousand rare birds, mammals, snakes, fish, and others. But no other dragons. That seems a shame in a world that was once rich in dragons.

5

AN UNFORGETTABLE SERPENT

QUITE POSSIBLY there will never again be a day in the life of Peninsula, Ohio, even remotely like Sunday, June 25, 1944. At least, most of the older citizens of that quiet little Ohio village hope such a day does not dawn again.

In the early morning, dairy farmers were getting the milking done. The housewives were in their kitchens fixing hot breakfasts. Many of the men had forsaken church on this special day. Instead they dressed in their field clothes and headed to town.

There they joined a growing throng of men, boys, and hound-dogs milling around in front of the barber shop. A look at the group was enough to frighten any peace-loving citizen. The group appeared to be a posse preparing to hunt to earth a public enemy.

Their weapons ranged through handguns, shotguns, rifles, pitchforks, and corn knives. There was much yelling and general confusion. Finally the police chief, Art Huey, began to outline his plan.

All of the men were to spread out in a line. Then they would start tramping along the banks of the Cuyahoga River, being careful not to overlook ravines and gullies and such hiding places as log piles and old junked automobiles. Hopefully one of them would spot the critter and give the signal. Then everyone up and down the line would converge on the victim, and heaven only knows what might occur. By this time the object of their hunt had gained widespread fame. As they set forth they were trailed by assorted photographers and reporters representing newspapers from many parts of the world.

The story had started when Clarence Mitchell was working in a field beside the river. Mr. Mitchell often was followed to his fields by his dogs, but on this day the dogs seemed mighty nervous. They whined and whimpered. Finally they slipped off through the fields for home, leaving their master all alone.

Shortly after that Mr. Mitchell looked up from his work. There in plain view was what he thought must have been the biggest snake in the world.

Mr. Mitchell stood rooted to the spot. The reptile, big around as a watermelon, was headed for the river. It stretched out across an incredible length.

Around that part of Ohio there are no truly big native snakes. The largest one Mr. Mitchell would likely see is the pilot blacksnake. One five or six feet long and big around as a banana would be big for its kind. But this creature crawling in front of Mr. Mitchell was unbelievable. The snake was twenty-five feet long and might have weighed more than two hundred pounds.

Mr. Mitchell made no effort to stop the huge snake, or to engage it in combat. Understandably. "I watched," he reported simply. And while he watched, the huge snake slid down the riverbank and into the Cuyahoga. As it did so, Mr. Mitchell dropped his hoe and raced for home.

Subsequently, the snake was observed by a neighbor who was working in a field on the east side of the river. It came out of the stream and headed eastward. Both farmers repeated their stories of what they had seen. Many believed they had been out in the sun too long.

But around Peninsula the giant serpent continued to make its appearance. On one farm after the other it showed up. Those who did not see the reptile itself sometimes reported sighting the tracks.

Soon most people took the story seriously. Farm wives no longer let their children go into the fields to pick daisies. Men continuously glanced to all sides as they plowed their corn. Older boys, driving the cows in at milking time, ran them more than they usually did.

Meanwhile, in town, the great snake was about all anyone talked about. Increasingly, folks knew they would have to protect themselves somehow against this jungle menace that had invaded northern Ohio. Such a beast simply could not be permitted to slither around the woods and fields. The chief of police was worried that some of his neighbors, nervous because of the reports of the monster serpent, might shoot each other by mistake.

What kind of snake might this Peninsula giant have been? There are in the world six true giants among the snakes. All belong to the same family of reptiles, the Boidae. Even herpetologists who spend their lives studying the snakes of the world, have had trouble arriving at a decision about which of these is truly the largest. They agree, however, that it must be either the anaconda or the reticulate python. Presently the record for the reticulate python is 33 feet from nose to tip of tail. But there is a believable record of an anaconda that measured 37.5 feet. This leaves the anaconda, as Clifford H. Pope, an outstanding authority on the subject, has written "probably *the* giant among the giants."

The boa constrictor, a little one among the giants, may go to 18.5 feet. The boa constrictor, however, is the best known of the giant serpents. It is often kept in captivity. The home of the boa is Mexico and South America.

The anaconda is also a native of South America. There it stays much of the time in the warm water, moving slowly about the dense jungle streams.

The other four giants are all pythons native to the Old World. One often housed in zoos is the African rock python which can grow to more than thirty feet in length. This snake is sometimes seen in the grasslands, its head lifted above the level of the vegetation as it examines the countryside. It is native to most of southern Africa.

Across southeastern Asia the Indian python is frequently found in the jungles as well as the grasslands. It may grow to be twenty feet long. Meanwhile the reticulate python crawls through the Philippine Islands, Burma, and other parts of that humid tropical region. The other monstrous snake in the line-up is also a python, the amethystine python. Sometimes this beast, whose length may go to twenty-two feet, departs its haunts along the stream banks to come into the villages and farms. It is a native to Australia and some of the islands of the South Pacific.

All of these massive reptiles are non-poisonous. They have little need for poison. They can subdue their prey by wrapping the hapless creature in masses of snake coils and hugging it to death.

Such snakes often lurk along trails used by wild hogs, antelope, and other animals. They choose what they like from the creatures that parade by. Or they may lie silently and deathly still along the limb of a giant tree that branches out over a jungle stream, ready to drop on their victims.

In ambush the giant snakes test the air for odors. They are also equipped with heat-sensitive organs which aid them in detecting the presence of warm-blooded creatures.

When hungry, the giant snake grabs its victim first with its jaws. The teeth curve backward. The harder a victim pulls to escape, the more deeply it is impaled and the more securely it is held. Then the snake quickly brings coils of its massive body around the animal. The opportunities to escape at this point are slight.

Some believe these huge constrictors break a multitude

of bones in their victims' bodies as they hold them. This is not the case. These big snakes do not squeeze their prey with great force. With their bulky coils wrapped about the struggling creature they just hold on. Each time the prey exhales, the snake takes up the slack, making it impossible for the victim to expand and draw in fresh supplies of oxygen. It soon suffocates.

Strangely, these reptiles are capable of eating animals even larger around than their own bodies. The jaws are flexible and loosely connected. They can adjust to the situation and spread around the large prey.

The swallowing process may be a slow one. Bit by bit, the reptile inches forward, stretching its own body over that of its victim. It pulls itself onto the prey somewhat as a person might force an elastic stocking onto his leg. The snake may enter an enclosure, capture, and consume a pig or calf, then find that it is too bulky to escape through the opening by which it entered.

How big an animal can a big snake swallow? There is one report from South Africa of a python 16 feet long swallowing an impala weighing 130 pounds. In South America an anaconda once consumed a five-foot cayman, an alligator-like reptile.

Meanwhile, one Indian python is credited with making a main course of an adult leopard. The snake is said to have suffered some scratches in the process. Serves him right.

On record also are authentic cases of reticulate pythons consuming people. Four Burmese hunters once went into the jungle in pursuit of game. Along the trail they became separated from each other. When they reassembled there were not four but three. This alarmed the remaining three. They straightway set forth searching for their missing friend.

First they found his sandals beside the trail. The sandals looked as if their owner had been lifted out of them. Soon the three men found a trail of broken vegetation. Then, resting in the shadows beside the trail, they found a python at least twenty feet long. Near its middle the great serpent's body was suspiciously bulky. The beast was slain upon the spot, and a post-mortem was soon performed. The lost hunter had been found. Somewhat late.

It would, however, be unfair to the giant snakes to imply that they often seek humans for their prey. They have distinct preferences for other warm-blooded species. In fairness, it should be noted that people also eat pythons.

All of this, however, is lost on people who find they have a giant reptile in their neighborhood. Around Long Beach, California, some years ago, there was instant pandemonium when word spread that the twenty-eight-foot-long python had escaped from a traveling carnival. The reptile was soon captured near the beach. That put an early end to the possibility of a scene such as the natives of Peninsula, Ohio, enacted at the time of their great snake hunt.

Every few days the snake would be seen again around the northern Ohio community. It would then slide into the brush and out of sight. By the time a posse could be organized and reach the site, the nervous hunters would find only mashed down grass, and more big tracks. This led to the big Sunday hunt in late June.

Nobody recalls for certain how many men and boys gathered to search for the serpent. The telephone operator was alerted to pass the word if anyone should call in a report of the monster. The local fire station was expected to sound three blasts of the siren on top the town hall.

The siren sounded about noon. Just about everyone who had not already gone out on the hunt now began to join in the chase. They didn't know it then, but the caller had spread a false alarm.

They searched every ravine and kicked every brush pile. They looked into the branches of trees over the river. They poked into holes. But all day there was no sign of the Peninsula python. Everyone went home tired that night. No one had been shot. Police chief Art Huey let out a sigh of relief. Perhaps so did the Peninsula python.

Where did the monster reptile come from? How did it get free halfway around the world from its native land? Folks in northern Ohio thought about that quite a bit. They recalled the day a carnival truck went out of control down by the cemetery. Everything that was inside it had spread over an acre or more. One of the things in it was believed to have been a giant python.

By autumn the python had vanished. Naturalists from Cleveland and from other cities speculated that it might have holed up for winter along the banks of the Cuyahoga and failed to survive the frigid northern Ohio weather.

6

AN OCTOPUS TO REMEMBER

ONE BEHIND THE OTHER, the waves roll in from the broad Atlantic and wash onto the sand beaches of Florida. Then the waters spread out in thin sheets and finally slip back to the ocean.

Behind them, in the darkness, they leave an offering for those who will walk the beach the next morning. Usually the waters carry only small creatures—the shells of angel wings, pearl whelks, and sand dollars. Shell collectors pick up these beautiful little gifts of the sea, admire them, then carry them home in brown paper bags. Meanwhile the waves continue, for the offerings from the sea are endless.

But one black night, in addition to little shells, the waves carried a startling burden. Each advancing wave moved the giant corpse closer and closer to shore. Gradually the waters below the corpse grew shallower. Finally the lifeless tentacles, dangling loosely, touched bottom and scraped along the sands.

By daylight the waves had lost much of their size and force. The whitecaps were gone, and only the gentlest waves continued to lap up against the sandy shores.

As the light grew stronger a strange shapeless form could be seen heaped upon the beach. By now it had no head and its legs were only stumps. It resembled what some people believed at first to be a dead elephant. But it was obviously of the sea.

Early strollers on the beach came upon the sea monster and stood around it in wonder. Not even in their worst nightmares had they seen such a creature as this.

One of the first scientists to study it and venture an opinion on its identity, according to F. G. Wood writing in *Natural History* magazine, was Professor A. E. Verrill of Yale University. The professor was known world-wide as an authority on giant squid of the ocean depths. But what Professor Verrill suggested about the monster lying lifeless on the St. Augustine beach sounded farfetched. He thought at first that it might be a giant octopus.

But the more he thought about this the more unlikely the whole idea seemed. Finally he declared publicly that he had changed his opinion.

This was understandable. After all, there was no such thing as a giant octopus known to science. If there were it would surely rank among the world's most frightening creatures.

By our standards there is not much that is pretty about

an octopus. Many people call them "devilfish." The octopus looks as if it might have been put together in the dark of the night from odds and ends. Even so, the average octopus, full grown, is a gentle soul with a body about the size of an orange.

Sticking out like bumps on the sides of the head are large eyes that allow the octopus to see well in the shadowy depths. It has a short neck by which the head is attached to a strange-looking body. The mouth is lined with strong jaws outfitted with horny material allowing the octopus to crush fish, crabs, and lobsters.

Assembled around its mouth are eight legs or arms, depending on your point of view. They are long, tapering, flexible tentacles. The legs of the octopus are remarkable. Along the underside of each one are two rows of suction cups. With these the octopus can get a firm grip on rocky ledges. In this manner, he moves along in what, to an octopus, may be walking.

This suction cup movement, however, is low-speed travel. If the octopus gets into real trouble, he has a couple of tricks in reserve. First he goes into high gear in reverse. This is accomplished much the same as the squid does it. He draws water into his body through a funnel-shaped opening beneath his head, then, he squeezes water back out through this siphon and becomes a squirt gun. The force of the water sends his body scooting backward through the depths. This is a good thing for an octopus to know, especially when he encounters a shark or other predator with a fondness for octopus meat. At the same time the octopus can force out of its body a black cloud of inky liquid that hides his movements. If these tricks are not sufficient, the octopus can change colors. Right before the eyes of a predator, the octopus may slip into his best green, white, or pink outfit depending on which color will make him match the surrounding rocks.

With all these good features going for him even the adult octopus is still frequently caught and consumed by various octopus eaters. He makes the chase as difficult as possible for big predators by living in crevices and holes among the rocks. In addition, the octopus is very cautious.

Among those who delight in eating octopus meat are people. The portion eaten is the legs. This is understandable, because an octopus is mostly legs. Besides, one octopus has as many legs as four chickens.

The octopus, marvelously camouflaged, can fit into odd-shaped holes in the rocks because he has no skeleton. He can fold up in any direction he chooses. He belongs to the cephalopods, the same group of animals as the squid.

In the salt-water world of the octopus the breeding season begins when a male and female come together for mating, and once the mating is accomplished the female is ready to lay fertile eggs. They are usually small, transparent, and grouped in clusters. The Atlantic octopus may keep producing eggs until she has 180,000 of them. Then she must tend them until they hatch. She takes this job so seriously that she does not eat. For two months she stands watch. Then, if all has gone well, there emerge from the eggs a whole family of tiny baby octopuses shaped just like their parents. Only then can the mother octopus break her long fast and begin to feed again.

Around the world there are octopuses living in every ocean. They are especially abundant in tropical waters. Scientists have identified about 140 species. The biggest one is often said to be *Octopus dofleini* of the North Pacific, a creature sometimes capable of spreading its arms out over a span of 20 feet or so. Even this monster would have seemed small if placed alongside the heap of flesh that washed out on the St. Augustine beach.

Many people prefer not even to think about the octopus, and especially a fantastic one huge enough to capture a fisherman and sink his boat. The vision is enough to bring a sailor out of his bunk screaming in the dark of night and swearing off rum toddies. No wonder Professor Verrill found his first observation difficult to believe.

What he might not have known was that native fishermen in some parts of the world have long spoken about giant octopuses living in the depths of the oceans. Around the Caribbean Sea, such creatures are considered fact by fishermen who claim to have seem them alive and speak ominously of such monsters reaching into fishing boats to extract fishermen.

As the strange creature lay dead upon the sand, newspaper headlines around the country speculated about it. There was no question that it was a monster. One look proved that much. But there are monsters and there are monsters. Precisely what this one might be was baffling.

For more than two months the great black bag of flesh lay there decaying beneath the Florida sun. Samples of it were taken and shipped off to the Smithsonian Institution and the museum at Yale University.

Once or twice the creature was moved. One time an investigating scientist using a dozen men and block and tackle, stretched it out the better to measure it. The remaining parts measured twenty-one feet long, and weighed an estimated six tons. As the creature continued to weather in the tropic air the hide grew so tough that an ax would not penetrate its three-inch-thick skin, but would instead simply bounce off.

Three quarters of a century after those samples went off to the Smithsonian, men of science still debated about the giant creature. Dr. Joseph F. Gennaro, Jr., a biologist, prepared microscope slides of sections of the tissue, then compared these with known samples of both octopus and the giant squid. Dr. Gennaro, who reported his conclusions in the pages of *Natural History*, believed the St. Augustine monster to be the remains of the biggest octopus ever measured.

How big would such an octopus be as it lived along the rocky ledges of the deep, clear Caribbean waters? Those arms were judged to have measured one hundred feet in length. From the tip of one tentacle to the tip of an opposing one it could have stretched across two hundred feet of ocean.

The possibilities that the last individual of a vanishing giant species might have washed up on the Florida shore seems unlikely. If there was one, there must have been others, and perhaps even bigger.

Octopus lovers assure us that the octopus is basically a gentle creature. But it is one thing to feel affection for a small octopus, and quite another to think kindly of one with eyes as big as dinner plates and a reach of two hundred feet.

The debate about the identity of the St. Augustine monster continues. While some insist that it was indeed an octopus, other authorities disagree. One of these with whom I talked recently was Dr. Gilbert L. Voss, renowned authority on cephalopods at the Rosensteil School of Marine and Atmospheric Science, University of Miami. Dr. Voss assured me that he does ". . . not believe a word of it." He carefully explained the differences in various marine creatures that might have washed up on the beach and spoke of the speed with which the soft body of the octopus decomposes when exposed to the elements. The St. Augustine creature had become exceedingly tough instead. Dr. Voss believes that it must have been the remains of either a whale or a shark which have accounted for stories of sea monsters before.

In a sense, it is too bad that the men of science do not solemnly agree that the creature was indeed a giant octopus. Without such a monster the depths of the sea lose some of their mystery. One might like to know that down there somewhere there really is an octopus with a two-hundred-foot reach, providing, of course, one did not come face to face with it.

7

JET-PROPELLED MONSTER

ONE HAS ONLY to close his eyes to imagine the gentle swelling of the midnight sea. So thick is the darkness that the thin line between sky and water is gone. The wind has gentled and died. The seas lie glassy. For the castaway adrift in a small boat, what form would the most frightening monster imaginable take at such an hour? Look over the side and into the depths.

There below, shapeless and changing in form, it moves slowly. Around its body there is a cold glow. The phosphorescent monster slowly takes shape as it rises toward the surface beneath the boat.

What form of life can this be? Such a creature must not be real at all, but simply born of imagination. Its eyes are giant lenses ten inches across. It has a body and head which seem formed all in one strange pulpy lump.

At the back of the long body is a tail, shaped like the tip of a spear. But the head is the most frightening part of all. In front of those eyes the face separates into ten long boneless arms, each curling and twisting in different directions as if feeling the sea for prey. Two of the arms are much longer than the others. They reach far ahead, into the water, exploring, touching, searching.

Along the underside of each fleshy arm are rows of suction cups, some as big as saucers, and capable of clamping onto some hapless prey and holding it tightly long enough to bring it to the mouth.

There the prey, lost in that jungle of entangling arms, is crunched between horny plates and swallowed.

What if this monstrous apparition were to slip one of those giant tentacles up and over the little boat drifting on the ocean's dark surface? This, we are assured, could happen. Such creatures as we have described do live in the ocean depths.

Some readers will recall from the laboratory sessions of biology courses that the creature here described is very like a squid. Most squid are small. But many a small animal when viewed under a magnifying lens becomes a monster. The squid, lying inert in the biology laboratory, awaiting the student's scalpel, is harmless enough in spite of its strange shape. From tip to tip it may measure eight inches and be about two inches across the body. The flimsy tentacles of this little sea creature seem harmless.

Such average-sized squid are collected by the millions

in nets along the Atlantic Coast. They are sometimes sold as bait to fishermen.

This salt-water animal is without a skeleton, a member of the *Cephalopoda*. The cephalopods are creatures that have no external shells and usually have the mouth surrounded with a circle of arms. One cousin of the squid is the octopus.

But the squid is a speedy character compared with cousin octopus. While the octopus crawls about the rocks, seeking prey, the squid cruises the open waters, chasing down whatever he chooses to eat. He can quickly overtake various species of fish.

The squid has two speeds, fast and slow, depending on whether he moves forward or backward. He travels forward at slow speeds by the movement of fins. But when the squid goes into reverse, he employs the principle of jet propulsion. Water taken in is forced out with such speed that his torpedo-shaped body rockets backward through the sea.

If the squid is pursued, it escapes by this high speed procedure. Meanwhile, it sends out, not plain transparent sea water, but a cloudy mass of black ink, a murky curtain that hides its escape route.

As we have said, there is nothing truly frightening about the average little squid, especially when it lies dead upon the laboratory table. But over the ages there have been reports of squid so large that they have taken people for food, and these reports cannot be ignored in any discussion of monsters.

Centuries ago, sailors returning from their voyages spoke

of such monsters of the sea. Often they were ignored or ridiculed. Men still ridicule "monster" stories. We tend to believe so strongly in our own full knowledge that there is little room for admitting new creatures, especially if they are unusual in size, shape, or form. Learned men have sometimes insisted that unless they already knew of such a creature it simply could not exist. This, as Dr. Bernard Heuvelmans explains so ably in his authoritative book *In the Wake of the Sea Serpents*, was for long years the fate of the giant squid.

During the 1700s Eric Pontoppidan spoke of giant sea creatures in his book *The Natural History of Norway*. He spoke of objects protruding from the surface of the sea and said, "It seems these are the creature's arms, and, it is said, if they were to lay hold of the largest man-o-war, they would pull it down to the bottom. After this monster has been on the surface of the water a short time, it begins slowly to sink again, and then the danger is as great as before, because the motion of this sinking causes such a swell in the sea, and such an eddy or whirlpool, that it draws down everything with it."

Over the years men of the sea carried back other tales of strange giant beasts cruising the depths. Men of science continued to grin and shake their heads in disbelief.

Gradually, however, bits of evidence more concrete were being offered. In the autumn of 1861 a French naval craft in the North Atlantic encountered an island of flesh floating on the surface. The ship's captain, having little else to do at the time, and being curious as well, decided that he would capture the slowly moving creature.

Guns were readied. Firing began. But nothing would penetrate that slippery leathery covering. Projectiles sank in, bounced back, then slid off into the sea. This can be frustrating to the captain of a gunboat. There was still one more weapon, the harpoon.

As the ship closed on the creature, swimming slowly because of a probable sickness, the harpooner aimed and released the weapon. The point was deeply imbedded in the sacklike body.

Finally, when the animal had been dragged closer to the ship, its flesh was pierced again and a line run through the back end of the body. Next the crew began winching the massive weight upward toward the deck. The line, however, cut through the flesh like a thread drawn through jello, and it appeared that the beast would slip back into the depths. To prevent this, a loop was thrown around the tail fin and, although the tail fin broke from the body under the force of the winch, the crew did manage to bring about forty pounds of the tail aboard. This evidence was taken eventually to the French Academy of Sciences.

What had the men aboard the gunboat seen? They knew all right what they had found whether anyone cared to believe or not. It was a giant squid. From the end of its tentacles to the tip of its other end it measured perhaps twenty-four feet in length, with a body alone that was perhaps eighteen feet long. It floated there in plain view before the crew. This was still not as large as the giant squid is likely to grow.

In 1847 one of the papers that had been read at a meeting of the Society of Scandinavian Naturalists concerned the giant squid. Six years later, with the subject still very much on his mind, the author of that paper heard of a giant squid washed up on the beach. A squid, once it runs aground, is helpless, no matter how much it exercises its jet power. Without the sea to support its bulk, it struggles until it perishes. A portion of the grounded giant reached the laboratory of the scientist who further described it and then gave it a scientific name, *Architeuthis monachus*.

Stories of monsters, like stories of any kind, have the tendency to change when passed from person to person. Few storytellers have ever been known to shrink a monster. Perhaps stories of the giant squid pulling themselves from the sea on dark nights, and crawling into the rigging of ships, toppling and sinking them, are fiction. But there can be no question that the biggest of the squid reach weights that total many tons.

One of the largest of recorded giant squid washed up on a beach in 1924. Much of the mutilated specimen was gone but the fact that it had possessed ten arms confirmed its identity. The body, which was nine feet thick, would have been higher, even lying on its side, than the ceiling of an average room. Scientists believe this specimen to have been more than one hundred feet long, not measuring the two long tentacles. From tip to tip, measuring the two long tentacles, it might have stretched through the sea for more than two hundred feet, two-thirds the length of a football field.

There is a more recent story, of a giant squid that took an entire ship into its grasp. One night the squid climbed upon the side of the ship. The captain found the ends of its tentacles along the deck. One tentacle grasped the ship's stern. Then the captain walked to the other end of his ship and there was another tentacle. The ship was 175 feet long. Dr. Ann Bidder, formerly of the Cambridge University Zoology Department, has said that such a creature would have a body at least 25 feet long. Dr. Bidder also added that she believed the story, and told other scientists that the ship's officer had an excellent reputation as a careful observer and accurate reporter of what he saw at sea. This squid would have a reach of more than 200 feet.

There are apparently authentic reports of giant squid capturing men. The fate of the unfortunate man can be assumed. The squid has no reason for capturing anything except to eat it. Divers must sometimes think of these stories as they explore the depths. And so must all who are adrift in small craft at sea. Sailors have reported saving themselves by quickly chopping off the groping tentacles that reach out of the sea and into fishing boats.

FEATHERED MONSTERS

WHEREVER EARLY EXPLORERS TRAVELED, they discovered creatures new and strange. Sometimes these wild beasts and birds were so different that they were scarcely believable. Consider, for example, the dodo. The first Europeans to find them were Portuguese sailors who came to the island of Mauritius in 1507. They are believed to have returned several times through the years. Then in 1598, Commander Jacob van Neck cruised along the shores of this island east of Madagascar.

There were no Europeans living here, nor, for that matter, on the two neighboring islands. The commander dropped anchor and went ashore to explore.

Deep forests shaded much of the island. Whatever else they found on this island, the strangest creature of all was

a remarkable bird that looked as if it had been designed
by a prankster playing a joke on naturalists.

The bird weighed about fifty pounds. It stood on short,
yellow legs and had a somewhat round-shaped body. Its
wings were small; they would not begin to lift that great
weight from the ground. Its tiny tail was a curled plume,
standing up like a little feather duster. The bird's head
was dominated by its bill, nine inches long, thick, and
hooked on the end. Unlike the crow or jay, this bird
seemed slow-witted, not very bright at all. This shortcom-
ing was hidden behind a comical look on its face.

Apparently, however, this bird had no need for bril-
liance, any more than it had a reason to fly. It faced no
natural enemies of consequence. So, what did it matter if
it stumbled clumsily and toppled over itself when running
through the forest? Neither did it matter if its low-hanging
undercarriage dragged on the ground.

Some believe the big, clumsy bird was named because
of its call. Sailors who first discovered it, claimed that it
said "dodo."

Wherever people encounter wild creatures, they have a
tendency to ask immediately what good such animals might
be to people. This test was, at once, applied to the dodo.
For all its strange design, the bird was larger than a swan
and looked to its discoverers like a lot of fresh meat packed
into one bird. The dodo bird proved extremely easy to kill,
an advantage to sailors but not to dodos. All a dodo hunter
had to do was stay out of reach of that stout bill while
striking the bird a fatal blow on the back of its head with

a club. For the first time in its recent history the big bird had met an enemy capable of coping with a dodo.

Back on ship with the dead birds, the crew waited while the cook stewed the prize. Each of the birds was three times as heavy as a turkey. Only a few would be needed to feed the entire crew.

The dodo which had proved easy to kill, however, was far more difficult to chew. According to Commander Van Neck's writings, the longer it had simmered in the pot, the tougher it seemed to be. Whether this is to be blamed more on the dodo than the cook no one will ever know, because both have now been gone for a few hundred years. Later, however, others who cooked dodos claimed their flesh to be tasty and tender.

It is said that once a year these birds produced a single white egg and incubated it on a platform of grass.

Likewise it is said that the dodo used the wings, which were no good for flying, for fighting instead. As they rushed upon each other, the pounding of their wings against the flesh of their neighbors resounded through the forests like claps of thunder. One species is said to have been equipped with a ball-like bone on each wing, and to have used these as a kind of war club during territorial struggles with others of its kind.

Quite likely people back in Europe would not have believed the commander as he described the dodo bird he had discovered. There was but one answer. He must carry one back, then no one could scoff. So Commander Van Neck proudly escorted the first dodo ashore in Europe in 1599. The ponderous bird, fat and unbelievable, soon became a favorite wherever it was displayed. In the following years others were taken to zoos in Europe.

Meanwhile, artists of the day, seeking fresh subject matter, painted the dodo in numerous pictures. As events turned out it is good that they did.

Mauritius, where the dodo was first seen by man, lies off the coast of Madagascar. In addition, there is the nearby Reunion Island which had a dodo of its own, and Rodriguez Island which had another dodo-like occupant called the solitaire. They were discovered about the same time and were all then in line for the same fate.

Less than half a century after its first discovery, the dodo of Mauritius was in for serious trouble. In 1644 Holland sent colonists to establish homes and farms on Mauritius. With them went hogs, dogs, cats, and people, all of which would consume dodos and their young or eggs. Hogs are especially destructive to ground-nesting birds, and free-running dogs must have worried, chased, and killed the stumbling dodos.

Then the dodo was gone from Mauritius. It is believed to have become extinct about 1681. Then soon it was also extinct on the neighboring island of Reunion. It may have persisted a while longer on Rodriguez, but the solitaires there were soon gone too. As dead as a dodo.

True, the dodo, dumb and ugly, never did have a lot going for it. It just went quietly about its island world, doing whatever dodos went about quietly doing. When it was gone, there was little evidence that it ever existed except in the pictures artists had painted in Europe.

As for mounted specimens, there was known to be only

one. It was in a private collection and was eventually transferred to the collection of a museum in Oxford, England.

There, when the staff was cleaning up the place one day, someone noticed the old stuffed dodo. What a ratty-looking specimen it was! The feathers were broken, rough, and out of place. Its general run-down appearance was enough to make a tidy museum staff feel shame and chagrin.

The staff looked at the tattered remnant and the museum director made his decision. "Take the bird out and dispose of it." So the last of the dodos was banished. But before it was fed into the flames the head and one leg, still in pretty good shape, were taken off and saved.

New evidence of what the dodo looked like came to light in the depths of a muddy swamp on Mauritius in 1865. That year a collection of dodo bones was found preserved in the mud. From these spare parts museum workers assembled skeletons of the bird. These became the foundations for restorations, or man-made dodos. Today, you may see in a museum what appears to be a preserved dodo, but it will be only the work of a clever taxidermist who has assembled a counterfeit model of one of the most remarkable big birds the world ever knew.

As big as it was, the fifty-pound dodo was a bit of a midget compared with another bird known to have lived on the island of Madagascar. Scientists studying bones and fossils have given this towering creature its name, *Aepyornis maximus*. It has also been called the "elephant bird." From what we know about "maximus" it seems safe to say that this was the largest bird ever to walk the earth.

A distant cousin of the ostrich and emu, the elephant bird is believed to have weighed half a ton. It stood on legs as thick as tree trunks and had a kick sufficient to drop a bull dead in its tracks. To be kicked to death by a bird would seem an ignoble way for a bull to depart.

Remarkable indeed was the egg of the elephant bird. It had a shell about as thick as a silver dollar and was so big it was used to hold water around the homes of native people living on the island. It would hold more than a gallon of liquid. *Aepyornis maximus* could have been forgiven for taking pride in such a magnificent egg.

Scientific interest in the bird ran high in the early 1600s. Naturalists believed they might yet find some alive. The French government appointed a governor of Madagascar, who was an observant naturalist interested in the remarkable world around him. Eventually he wrote a book of his experiences. In those pages he mentioned the bird with eggs so large they were used as water jugs, and added that he himself had seen such eggs. But a series of unfortunate events was to cut the story short.

First, when the governor was on his way back to France where naturalists might have asked him more about the elephant birds, he encountered a gang of pirates. They killed him.

Gradually the elephant bird slipped from conversation, memory, and scientific concern. Two hundred years passed. Then the story was revived. Traveling naturalists once more began to hear reports of the remarkable giant birds in the interior of Madagascar.

As interest mounted, efforts were made to collect the

eggs and bring them out to civilization where the light of science might shine upon them. But only one such egg was known to have been collected. It was on its way back to France when the ship transporting it sailed into a massive storm. The ship crashed upon the shoals and sank from sight beneath the waves, egg and all.

Then in 1848, a trader heard again of the giant birds, and was told that deep in the inland portions of the island, they still survived. But they have never been seen by scientists to this day. The last of the elephant birds is doubtless gone. With it went the last of a legendary species, the biggest birds that ever lived. There remains much that we shall never know about this feathered monster.

9

THE MONSTER THAT WAS
TOO GOOD TO LAST

OF ALL THE MONSTERS men have found, few could be more unusual than the one discovered two centuries ago in the frigid waters off the coast of Alaska. No person alive today ever saw one of these creatures. They were seen, however, by one of the most famous naturalists of those times. Except for his records, the world might not have the slightest idea today that the creature lived. And what a beast it was!

This strange ponderous mass of flesh and bones lived half submerged in the shallow waters by the edge of the ocean. Its world was one of rocky, barren islands, wrapped in fog and swept by bitter winds.

These islands are the Aleutians. They lie like a string of unpolished gems, stretched out across the northern waters for eleven hundred miles. Each of the Aleutian Islands is a peak of a submerged mountain whose base rests on the ocean floor. Together they form a barrier between the Pacific Ocean and the Bering Sea.

Today these islands are mostly uninhabited and nearly all lie within the Aleutian Island National Wildlife Refuge. They are the homes of countless thousands of sea birds that fly and glide around the cliffs and mountainsides. Here also live seals and sea otters, swimming in the shallow waters.

Until 1741 the islands were inhabited only by a group of Stone Age people related to the Eskimos and known as Aleuts. These people had lived there for thousands of years, taking their food from the sea. They considered the islands their ancestral homes and they knew their strange world better than any other people alive. But it is the nature of people to insist that a land is only discovered when people of their own kind find it. In 1741 foreigners "discovered" the Aleutian Islands and proclaimed that henceforth they owned them.

In that year the government of Russia had organized and outfitted a daring expedition. At the head of the group was Captain-Commander Vitus Bering. His two ships had crossed the turbulent straits propelled by the sea winds.

Bering's voyage was filled with hazards and heartache. The seas around these islands are often whipped up by strong threatening winds. Reefs of jagged rocks hide close to the surface. Bering's ships crashed upon the rocks. The men were stranded on an island now known as Bering Island.

Through the following months many members of the expedition died there far from their homes. Those healthy enough to work, began rebuilding one of the ships so they might eventually escape again to the comforts of Russia.

Among these survivors was the naturalist, Georg Wilhelm Steller. He would leave the only description of the monster these explorers found around the shores of Bering Island. Steller recorded his observations in his notes written in Latin and passed down to present-day scholars. For hour on hour, he sat huddled in the drizzling rain faithfully writing down descriptions of what he saw. And there must have been times when he scarcely believed it all himself.

In the Aleutians, there were animals new to science. Among Steller's remarkable discoveries were the sea otter, Steller's sea eagle, Steller's jay, and Steller's eider, a sea duck. But the creature that brought the young naturalist the greatest fame was the sea cow he and the rest of Bering's crew had found wallowing in the shallow beds of kelp along the coasts of these lonely islands. Steller wrote that these thirty foot mammals "live like cattle in the sea." They stayed in herds and seemed constantly to be eating.

To obtain food they wallowed along the shallows scraping seaweed from the rocks and munching it as they moved their large heads from side to side. Once in a while they would lift their heads out of the water for fresh air. Then they would snuff and snort and go right back to eating.

One day the ship's crew began looking hungrily at these giant beasts. The ship's food was gone. The sailors were weak from hunger. Often they were too weak and ill to continue working on the ship that was to carry them away from this forsaken land. If they could only capture one of those monsters swimming there so close by, they could soon learn if the creature was good to eat.

But how do you sneak up on a monster and catch it? This could be dangerous. The animals, according to Steller's estimates, weighed as much as four tons each.

Whenever high tide came the sea cows, as the sailors called them, would move in close to shore where they would go right on munching seaweed. Finally the sailors could resist temptation no longer. Instead of a fish hook they needed a monster hook, and they prepared an iron weapon that looked like a ship's anchor. Then they attached it to a rope. When this monster tackle was ready, a small crew moved off in a boat. Thirty men on shore held tightly to one end of the rope.

As the boat neared one of the huge animals, the heavy iron hook was lifted by one of the sailors and brought down with a long slashing blow. It hooked into the flesh of the giant animal. At that moment the sea began to erupt. The creature thrashed about in surprise and pain and the foaming waves threatened to swamp the little boat.

As the men on shore tugged and pulled, their companions in the boat attacked the monstrous sea mammal with every weapon they had. Other sea cows moved in to aid their stricken companion. Some of them tried to upset the bobbing dory by heaving the boat up on their backs. Others attacked the ropes that held the sea cow. They even tried to remove the hook from her back by striking it with their broad tails.

But the ship's crew eventually towed the weary, stricken animal to shore and began hacking large chunks of meat from its body. Beneath a four-inch layer of thick white fat there appeared red meat that reminded some of the sailors of beefsteaks. Sadly, whenever they would leave the scene the old cow's mate would come back to the shallows and linger close beside her dead body.

To Steller, the capture of one of these strange beasts meant more than food. The naturalist saw the event as a new scientific opportunity. For the first time, he could examine the body of a sea cow closely. He could study its structure. He could try to figure out where it belonged in the organization of the animal kingdom. He knew from the beginning that he had discovered one of the most unusual animals on earth.

He skinned and picked and poked at the mass of flesh. The front part was more like an animal that might live on land. In spite of its large head, the sea cow had tiny dark eyes perhaps no larger than those of a sheep. Time and evolution had given it a tail shaped much like that of a fish. Its body measured twenty-five feet in girth. Its skin was blackish brown, deeply wrinkled, and it seemed to wear a coat several sizes too large for it. The stomach of one such animal that Steller dissected was six feet long, the heart weighed thirty-six pounds, and the liver had to be cut up to be moved.

On other days Steller studied the actions of these monsters. For ten months he studied them. The cows, he concluded, had no more than one calf each year, and it was his belief that the adults chose mates for life and formed strong family groups, which would seem to be as good a plan for sea cows as for anyone else.

Other ships followed Bering to these newly discovered islands. They were sent out to kill the sea otters and bring back shiploads of their fabulously rich fur. Over the next hundred years these hunters almost wiped out the sea otters which had once bobbed in the ocean in fantastic numbers around the Aleutian Islands.

The crews of these ships needed food and like Bering's men they looked upon the monstrous sea cows as fresh meat. The sea cows' numbers dwindled fast. In 1768 the last of them ever recorded was killed on Bering Island. Perhaps it was the last sea cow on earth. Only twenty-seven years had passed since the creature was discovered. The remarkable monsters had been quickly ushered into extinction.

Looking over the roster of the earth's creatures we find that Steller's sea cow had some distant relatives. Some of its smaller cousins still live. Perhaps best known of these "little" cousins is the Florida manatee, which today is also threatened with extinction.

Like Steller's sea cow, the manatee has no hind limbs, and its forelimbs have gradually changed into flippers. It lives in the warmest waters of Florida, around the edges of the Everglades National Park and in nearby canals. Once it ranged all the way along the coast to North Carolina and westward to southern Texas. Hunting, and the constantly changing habitat, however, have taken toll of this half-ton mammal. Today it is well on the road to extinction. It may soon join its long gone cousin that lived in the chill waters of Alaska.

Explorers have also found other relatives of these big clumsy swimmers in other parts of the world. Three species of manatees were identified. There were also three species of the related dugong, one each from the Red Sea, Australia, and the Indian Ocean.

Scientists studying fossils concluded that they were land animals, perhaps fifty million years ago. In those times the ancestral creature lived part of the time on land and part in the water. But over the ages it spent increasing amounts of its time in water. Its body adapted and evolved, gradually acquiring the form of the manatee and the sea cow. It became a massive leathery bag of blubber and flesh, shaped half like a mammal and half like a fish.

In this form the sea cow was doing very well. It had become a highly successful monster. But monsters, we now know, come in all sizes. And as big as they were, these monsters by the edge of the sea proved no match for the man-sized creatures that were to discover them.

10

AN INCREDIBLE SEARCH

To Dr. James P. Chapin nothing could have been more exciting than the discovery of a wild creature never before known to science. Over much of his adult life Dr. Chapin had wandered through the dense jungles of the Congo. There was no man who knew the birds of the Belgian Congo better. He knew them so thoroughly that he was busy writing a two-volume set of books on the subject.

Of these, the first book was already completed. The second was well underway. Then suddenly there came the hint that he might have missed a large, living Congo bird and left it out of the first volume completely. This was unbelievable. The events that led up to the final chapter of this search have been recorded by Dr. Chapin himself.

His search and discovery is one of the all-time classics in the annals of scientific detective work.

From the time he was a boy Chapin was interested in birds. While other children were content to chase chickens, James was studying their feathers. He found that the feather of a bird is one of the truly amazing structures in the natural world. This awakened in his mind an interest that followed him throughout his life and into distant corners of the world.

Eventually he completed his scientific schooling, and joined the staff of The American Museum of Natural History in New York City. His first big foreign adventure came in 1913.

That year he went into the heart of Africa as an assistant on a scientific expedition. During those months in the Belgian Congo young Dr. Chapin studied feathers of many strange birds he was seeing for the first time. One day he took special notice of the headdress of a native from the Ituri forest. The man wore on his head a couple of feathers like none Dr. Chapin had ever seen before. Dr. Chapin bought them from the tribesman.

When he returned to New York in 1915, he carried a bundle of feathers. Among the museum trays of birds he identified these feathers, one after the other, by comparing them with those of known birds. He labeled them as he made his identifications.

But two of the feathers in his bundle were like nothing else he could find among the thousands of birds in the museum. These were the large feathers the native hunter had worn on his head. Dr. Chapin was puzzled by this mystery. He could not find the answer.

Years passed. Dr. Chapin continued his studies of the Congo birds. When he was not deep in the jungles, he added to his book. But unsolved riddles are not easily forgotten by the scientific mind.

Then in 1936 Dr. Chapin left New York again. This time he sailed for Europe and the Congo Museum near Brussels, Belgium. He was no stranger around this museum either. At various times during the previous fifteen years he had studied the birds there, nearly all of them from Africa.

Shortly after reaching the Congo Museum, Dr. Chapin was walking one day from his own laboratory to the office of the museum director. But he took a slightly different route to the director's office on this day than he ever had before. As he later wrote in *Natural History* magazine, his route took him, ". . . by pure chance . . . through a corridor I had never before entered. It was here that my eyes fell on the two mounted pheasants, standing on top of a cabinet."

Dr. Chapin stood rooted to the spot. His mind raced back across twenty-four years to the day an African tribesman with two strange feathers in his hair stood before him. Those feathers had been reddish brown, with black bars on them. The feathers, still unidentified, waited in a museum cabinet. Dr. Chapin believed they had come from some gallinaceous, or chicken-like bird. He recalled that at the time he thought they might be from some bird unknown to science. But he had dismissed that idea as "preposterous." Of that moment as he stood before the two mounted specimens, he said later, "Now I had stumbled on the bird from which it must have come."

Dr. Chapin rushed on to the office of the director and questioned him about the two dusty mounted birds standing neglected on top of the hall cabinet. He had already inspected their labels and knew they were not correctly identified. They were not peacocks as the tags said. Where, he wanted to know, had they come from? How had they reached the Congo Museum?

The two "peacocks" had arrived at the museum as part of a collection of mounted birds from a Brussels business firm. For many years they had stood on display in cases in the company office. The big question was where these mystery birds had been killed, and Dr. Chapin could only speculate on this.

Then, about a month later, he was invited to dine with a gold mining engineer known to him from his days in the Congo, a quarter of a century before. The engineer recalled from his experience in the Congo a dinner he had been served in 1930 in the heart of Africa. One of the natives had brought in the bird which the engineer now described for Dr. Chapin.

As he spoke of the bird's form and feathers, Dr. Chapin was thinking of the mounted and mislabeled "peacocks" in the museum. His excitement was growing. His host then drew a sketch of the Congo bird, and it was plainly a picture of the museum's unidentified birds. With this, all doubts were gone, and as Dr. Chapin wrote, ". . . we were dealing with a great discovery, a typical pheasant with some slight resemblance to the Asiatic peacocks."

This was all the more amazing because there were no other known members of the true pheasant family in all of Africa.

But for Dr. Chapin the search was only getting underway. Several years had passed since the engineer friend had feasted on the strange bird. Next, the world of science would have to find the birds living in the wild Congo forests. Only then would the strange search be completed and the proof be absolute.

This would mean another trip to the Congo to search for the newly discovered bird, and Dr. Chapin began at once to plan such a journey.

Had others seen the strange "new" bird, or heard about it? Dr. Chapin wrote a brief article and it was reprinted in Africa. Such an announcement is likely to bring in a wide variety of reports. Most people would like to play a part in the discovery of a new wild creature. Few, however, have the training or experience to know the common from the uncommon. Dr. Chapin expected to hear from people who mistook other birds for the Congo pheasant.

He did. But he also obtained a few leads that he knew he should follow. One came from a policeman who said that he had once shot one of the birds. What's more, he had the bird mounted. It was now in the possession of his sister in Belgium. In due time this specimen arrived at the museum and it was indeed one of the strange pheasants.

Finally, on the edge of the jungle country in the Congo, where he was certain the birds must live, Dr. Chapin began his own hunting. Friends had sent to him a skilled native hunter, a man who knew all the creatures of the woods including, he said, the strange pheasant which Dr. Chapin had come so far to find.

During the days that followed, the two men, one from America and the other from the Congo, walked through the forests alert for a sign of the bird. They stopped often to listen and look, and searched one forested slope after the other. The hours wore on and days passed. Then Dr. Chapin's luck turned for the better.

"The morning had been rainy," Dr. Chapin said, "the afternoon was very dark, and at 5:20 we had just started homeward. We were ascending a slope when I saw something dark running through the low bushes ahead."

His companion was carrying a gun for just such an occasion and he, too, glimpsed the dark form of the large bird. The man dashed off through the brush and Dr. Chapin saw him lift the gun. There followed the sharp explosion and sound reverberated through the woodlands. When Dr. Chapin saw the bird again, it had escaped and hurtled itself into the air. Now it pulled itself through the woods at top speed, and neither of the men ever saw it again. They soon saw a second bird and this one, too, escaped.

Two days later, when they were hunting, two birds flushed again, and this time the hunter dashed forward, then slowed, and began looking into the trees overhead. Then he quickly raised his gun and fired twin blasts. Dr. Chapin heard the heavy body of the bird thump against the ground. The hunter ran and brought it back even before it was dead.

For Dr. Chapin, the search that had started years earlier with two unknown feathers was now near its end. At last he held in his hand full proof, not only that these birds still lived, but also where they dwelled. The bird carried to him that day was a young male.

With one bird in possession perhaps he could press forward, continue the hunt and add still others to his collection. In those days ornithologists commonly looked upon rare birds as something one collected for museum shelves. In later times, with so many species becoming rare and threatened, scientific observers are far more inclined to allow the rare birds to go on living.

For another five days Dr. Chapin stayed in the forest hunting the Congo "peacock." But the only one he took was the single young male bird shot from its perch in the tree.

How could a bird so large have gone undetected by science for so long? This was a question Dr. Chapin was often asked. The answer, he felt, must lie in the fact that the bird's range had by then shrunk to remnants of what it once had been. As far as he could determine it was found only in the limited region of the Congo where ornithologists had not then done much research.

Since then, however, it has been located in numerous places through the Congo forests. The longer scientists studied the bird, the more clearly they realized that it was not truly as rare as Dr. Chapin's remarkably long search would indicate. It is not now considered either rare or endangered.

Besides, gallinaceous birds, to which the Congo pheasant belongs, are easily raised in captivity and a number of zoos far from the bird's native Congo now have stocks of these birds.

For all those who seek to unravel the threads of evidence running through the cloth of natural history, there is a lesson in the long trail followed by Dr. Chapin as he pieced together the story of the Congo "peacock." There are still mysteries to ponder, hidden trails to explore, questions to ask. No one can know for certain that all the strange creatures have yet been discovered. And the perpetual promise of another unknown keeps restless observers watching both sides of the trails as they walk and studying the feathers worn by native hunters they meet.

11

MYSTERIOUS TRACKS

TALLEST OF THE WORLD'S MOUNTAINS are the Himalayas. They extend for fifteen hundred miles across southern Asia. In some places the range is two hundred miles wide. Within this sprawling desolate region lie wilderness valleys and towering peaks seldom visited by men. There are also some fertile valleys, choked with dense jungle and dotted with little farm clearings. But farther up the climate grows cold, until finally the world is filled with snow-capped peaks, sharp ridges, and precipitous cliffs.

In this high country of the Himalayas, beyond 13,000-foot elevations, the elements are harsh and the wind blows bitter cold, stirring white laceworks of snow around the boulders. One might think that in this inhospitable world no large creatures could exist at all.

But what about those giant footprints? On numerous occasions mountaineers have discovered them. Something seems to go walking up there.

Colonel L. A. Waddel was exploring the slopes of Mt. Everest, the world's highest peak, in 1887. When he came down he reported unidentified footprints. Three years later another climber reported having seen the prints again. This time they were at an elevation of 18,500 feet. The tracks led uphill and vanished among the boulders. Russian soldiers reported shooting and killing such a creature in their mountain country in 1925.

Again, in 1942, Slavomir Rawicz, a Polish soldier escaping from a Russian concentration camp, was making his way back out over the Himalayas. As he crossed over from Tibet, he encountered, at a distance of only one hundred yards, two manlike creatures. He estimated them to be eight feet high and said they had massive arms, square heads, and were covered with thick coats of brown fur.

To Tibetan tribesmen these reports are not unexpected at all. They seem to know these are the creatures that have long lived there. They have various local names. Usually they are called "Yeti." More commonly, the rest of us call them "Abominable Snowmen."

What could they be? Maybe giant bears. Some insisted and even said they belonged to the species *Ursus arctos isabellinus*. But the Abominable Snowman, as proved by his footprints, walks on two feet. Bears can walk on two feet but do not do so for more than a few steps. They are definitely not known to go leaping about the snowfields on their hind feet.

Others claim that the mysterious tracks in the snow were left by a langur monkey. But these creatures are too small, and besides, they, too, walk on all four feet.

Meanwhile, doubters speculate that high altitude does strange things to people, and maybe some, frightened by the lonely place, let their imaginations run wild.

The trouble with this has been that over the years evidence continues to pile up indicating that the Snowman— or something—is up there just as the local tribesmen have always insisted.

One report tells of an Everest expedition of 1923. Far above them the climbers sighted figures in the snowfields. The creatures were moving. When climbers reached the area, there were the footprints showing plainly in the snow.

When Italian explorer A. N. Tombazi climbed up to the glacier area in 1925, one thing he definitely did not expect to encounter was the Abominable Snowman. At first, Tombazi had a tendency to make light of the whole story. When the subject came up in conversations he would flash his charming smile on those assembled and refer to the legendary Snowman as "that delicious fancy." But that was before Mr. Tombazi went up the mountain.

Somewhat later, back in Bombay, India, his story was quite different. He had seen his first Abominable Snowman. One of his excited porters drew his attention to it. "Unquestionably," Tombazi wrote later, "the figure in outline was exactly upright, and stopping occasionally to uproot some dwarf rhododendrons. It showed dark against the snow and wore no clothing." Later, he found the footprints and described them in detail.

Among others who had seen tracks was explorer and surveyor Eric Shipton. He found tracks at 16,000 feet in 1936. Later, in 1951, he found other tracks and photographed them. These pictures have helped convince many that there is substance to the story of the Abominable Snowman. The photograph showed a foot with four toes. Obviously it was not the foot of a bear. Neither was it anything else scientists could identify. ". . . these animals, whatever they were," said the New York *Times*, "did exist . . ."

At 19,000 feet, Sir John Hunt again found "Snowman" prints in 1937. Another story tells of two Norwegians who happened on two sets of tracks in that same area eleven years later. The Norwegians followed the tracks hoping for a look at the strange creatures about which they had heard and read. Soon they came upon the "Yeti," responsible for the tracks.

If you come back down the mountain and report having seen the "Yeti," some may believe. But if you bring along the Abominable Snowman, nobody can doubt your word. But what the Norwegians are said to have done next was not exactly the approved way of capturing an Abominable Snowman; they tried to lasso it. This effort failed and we are spared details of why or how. The Norwegians came back down the mountain and reported that the Abominable Snowman looks a lot like a large ape.

This description, however, is a generalization. What would the Abominable Snowman look like, if you should encounter one? Naturally there are variations in the reports by eye witnesses. No two people, surprised by a monster high in the Himalayas, are likely to see quite the same thing.

But the following composite portrait is assembled from various sources. Understandably, considerable attention has been paid to the feet. There have been reports of tracks up to eighteen inches long. But people of sound judgment now believe the feet of the Abominable Snowman to be somewhat smaller. Most agree that they are at least twelve to fourteen inches long and quite broad in proportion to their length. Those photographed by Eric Shipton were twelve inches long. They are so wide that in some tracks where the sun has melted the edges of the tracks they appear almost round or square.

However, smaller tracks have been found too, and this leads some people to speculate that there are actually two kinds of Yeti, a small species and a large one. The smaller species has been reported from time to time at lower elevations in the dense jungles of the river valleys. Along these rivers, when there is no snow, they leave their marks in the sands.

In the highlands, however, the Snowmen may appear suddenly anywhere between 13,000 and 20,000 feet. They seldom come down to the villages, just as people seldom go up to elevations where the Yeti live.

The Snowmen are covered with long brownish hair which falls down over their eyes. Their heads are said to be pointed on top and their eyes are deeply sunken and reddish. Their light-colored faces are without hair, we are told, and not at all pretty, except perhaps to another

Yeti. They do not have a tail. The feet, like most of the body, are covered with hair.

When the Everest Expedition was far up the mountains in 1921 their Tibetan porters told them about the food habits of the Yeti. These strange creatures, according to local legend, eat yaks and people. There seems little evidence to support this statement.

Strangely, some Tibetan people also believed that the Abominable Snowman has its feet on backward. The reason for this has never been fully explored. Maybe an Abominable Snowman can get turned around like anybody else.

Chances are excellent that the farther one lives from the land of the Abominable Snowman, the easier it is to make fun of stories about these legendary creatures. Travelers have long noticed that groups of people living in Tibet and Nepal suddenly become quiet and deeply troubled when the subject is brought up. One expedition of Russian scientists that set off to find the Yeti decided that the creatures do, in fact, exist. "Many tribesmen," said the official report, "have met the creature. They speak of it as an animal moving on two legs, with brown shiny fur and long hair on its head. Its face looks like both ape and man. Hunters often find remnants of its food, for example, bits of rabbit. But according to them, the wild man also eats plant roots."

Meanwhile, all who study the evidence must eventually consider the strange unidentified scalp owned by the monks in a monastery far up in the Himalayas near the border between Nepal and Tibet. If a visitor comes, and they like him, the monks may bring out and display the patch of hair. They have had it in their possession for perhaps three hundred years. Ask the monks what it is and you get a brief answer, "It is the scalp of a Yeti." How they obtained it from the Yeti is not recorded.

It is shaped like a scalp or hat. Unlike a hat, it has no seams and has never been sewed. One visitor, years ago, managed to remove a few of the brown hairs from the scalp. They were sent to New Jersey to be studied by a professor who was an authority on hair. But the scientist could not identify it. He knew of no other hair with which it would match.

What should you do if you meet an Abominable Snowman? The creature is, after all, experienced in getting around the rugged snowbound country, and can leap over boulders with the agility of a gazelle. The best defense, according to one regional story, is to quickly gather up as many rocks and sticks as you can. Then toss these treasures to the creature one at a time. With considerable skill, the Yeti will reach out and catch the objects. Soon both arms are filled.

At that point he seems not to know quite what to do. He is good at catching but reluctant to drop any of the newly acquired prizes, so he just stands there burdened down with rocks and stones while you run away down the mountainside. Perhaps, with greater exposure to the Abominable Snowman, people will someday work out a better defense.

There is, of course, much evidence that the Abominable Snowmen want only to stay away from people. They vanish into the brush or behind rocks. They prefer to stay at elevations far above people and usually at least two miles above sea level.

Explorers, besides Norwegians with lassos, have long dreamed of capturing a Yeti. But what in the world would one do with it? Although these may be primitive manlike creatures, as some seriously believe, we have every reason to suspect that they want no part of our cherished civilization. As we look about us, this is sometimes understandable. One can hardly imagine an Abominable Snowman in a traffic jam. He belongs to the vast, wind-swept, mountain slopes. There in the rugged snowfields, he goes right on leaving his strange tracks. Those who find them come down the mountain with a new sense of wonder. Perhaps up there in the high Himalayas, the mountain climber is not really as much alone as he might have thought.

12

SASQUATCH ALIAS "BIGFOOT"

From NORTHERN CALIFORNIA, through Oregon, Washington, and into British Columbia, the mountains are wild and deeply timbered. In this country there are new reported sightings every year of manlike monsters, huge, hairy, and indescribably ugly.

Indians of the Pacific Northwest knew about these giant, wild men of the forests hundreds of years ago. The Indians called them "Sasquatch." More recently, people, standing spellbound before fourteen-inch-long footprints, have called the monster "Bigfoot."

Each year more people than ever before are out there in the deeply wooded valleys hoping for a glimpse of the big-footed Sasquatch.

Where could such monsters have come from? They

could, some explain, have come from the same place the native Indians and Eskimos came from to settle North America. During the time of the Wisconsin glacial epoch the level of the oceans was lower. More of the world's supply of water was locked up in ice and snow. This exposed a wide bridge of land across the North Pacific connecting Asia and North America.

Across this land bridge came the ancestors of many wild creatures found here, deer, bear, bison, wild sheep, and others. Perhaps the people, moving a few miles at a time, followed these animals, which they hunted for food. And perhaps in those times there came as well some creatures we still know very little about.

Slipping along in the shadows of night may have been a tall, hairy creature looking more like people than like any of the other creatures around them. This could explain how the ancestors of Sasquatch first came to the forests of the Pacific Northwest; they came on their big feet. They would have come, you understand, from Asia, which is also home of the Abominable Snowman, presumably a cousin to Bigfoot. If these two manlike monsters differ in form and coloring today, this can be explained by evolution and adaptation to different environments. People need only look at themselves to understand that humans from various parts of the earth have their own physical differences.

It is likely that the creature we now know as Bigfoot was never abundant. Except for the fact that they have managed to stay out of sight of men so well, there might, by now, be none of them remaining.

Not until the 1950s did many people begin thinking seriously about the possibility that there might really be a Bigfoot. Then timber workers, in lonely logging camps of northern California, began finding strange giant tracks around their dwellings and beside the forest trails. Plaster casts of these prints were sometimes made and preserved. The story spread, and people began to ask each other if such human-shaped animals did live up there in the woods. Many believed they did.

Soon someone recalled a remarkable story that had appeared in Portland, Oregon, newspapers in 1924. On the east slope of Mount St. Helens lived a grizzled old prospector, all alone in his little cabin in the silence of the deep forest. On an August day he left his cabin and hurried off to search for a forest ranger. He told the foresters his strange tale.

"They woke me up in the middle of the night," he said, "throwin' stones at my place. Some of them stones was big ones, some even come through the roof. And all the time they was around the house, they was screaming like a bunch of apes. I didn't dare go outside. That's probably what they wanted me to do. Would you have gone outside? No sir! Instead I crawled under the bed, and I stayed there till morning come. Sometime in the night them critters quit their screamin' and slunk off in the dark. Next morning when I went outside there was the tracks, big ones, a foot or more across, and right up beside my place."

That story appeared in newspapers in Washington and Oregon. Soon the wooded slopes of Mount St. Helens were filled with nervous hunters. They were alert for the slightest noise, the big footprint, or a glimpse of a furry hide in the undergrowth. Considering the assortment of rifles, shotguns, and pistols they carried, it was a blessing nobody got shot.

They saw no sign of the Bigfoot. Gradually folks around those mountains seemed to forget the giant, hairy monsters again. Sasquatch was becoming more elusive than ever. He wanted very little to do with man and this was understandable, even to man.

But following the reports from the California logging camps, the story began growing again. In the years since, the evidence has piled up. More and more, people in the Pacific Northwest are convinced that something in human form, but not very human at all, really lives in the deepest and darkest forests. There is now a list of more than three hundred reported sightings of Bigfoot. Undoubtedly there would be more except for the elusive nature of the beast and its nocturnal habits. Still no Bigfoot has been captured or killed. Seldom has one been photographed. The most notable exception occurred in the mountains of northern California in 1967.

Roger Patterson lives with his wife and three children on the little horse ranch they operate near Yakima, Washington. For several years he had been studying the exploits of Bigfoot and figuring out the best place to go look for the creature.

On October 20, 1967, Mr. Patterson and his friend, Bob Gimlin, had been high in the mountains in northern California for almost a week. On that day Mr. Patterson says, ". . . when riding horseback up a creek bottom, we encountered this creature. My horse smelled it, jumped, and fell." Mr. Patterson scrambled for his saddlebag. "I got the camera out of the saddlebag," he says, "and ran across the creek and we were able to get twenty-nine feet of sixteen-millimeter colored film."

After three miles of tracking through rough country, the two men lost Bigfoot's trail in deep undergrowth. They made plaster casts of the footprints. Other people returned later and also saw and measured the 14½-inch prints.

This newly made film was sent down to Hollywood. There, experts in "special effects," men who really know how to set up a fake picture, studied and restudied Patterson's disturbing movies. Each of them decided that in no way could Patterson have faked his pictures.

Next the movies were shown to a lengthy list of scientists. Among them were noted zoologists. They arrived as doubters, but following a look at the Patterson movies, left "shaken." Of special interest to the zoologists was the movement of the muscles as the Bigfoot walked. This movement was proof enough to many that the creature was real and the Patterson movies authentic. The figure photographed, a female, walked upright like a human and measured about seven and a half feet tall, three feet across the shoulders, had arms three feet long, and weighed an estimated eight hundred pounds.

In addition to his movies, Patterson tells of other evidence that Bigfoot lives. In 1958 he interviewed Charles Cates, an aging man who had once served as mayor of

North Vancouver. Cates recalled three old Indians whom he considered reliable, and all of whom told of hairy giants they had seen in their youth. Perhaps there were more of the monsters around in those times. One of the Indians had been in a tent one night with friends when a Bigfoot stuck its hairy head through the tent door and looked in upon them.

Near Yankton, Oregon, according to Mr. Patterson's records, several people sighted the hairy giants in 1926. A truck driver swore that one of them had trotted along beside his logging truck looking into the cab at him.

In 1941, according to a report given Patterson by Mrs. George Chapman, she and her children saw "an eight-foot hairy man come out of the woods." The creature went into a lean-to behind their cabin. As it went in the back door, the Chapmans went out the front door. They fled into the forest. For a long time they huddled there in the shadows. When they returned to their home, huge tracks marked the place where the giant had walked. The deputy sheriff from Blaine, Washington, came out and made casts of the footprints. This Bigfoot had the biggest feet of all. They measured sixteen inches long. The Bigfoot tramped down a patch of potatoes as it departed for the forests.

Then the next year, near Eugene, Oregon, Don Hunter and his wife spotted a "giant biped" walking, taking long strides, over the mud flats of Todd Lake.

Such reports, when coupled with Patterson's movies, are not to be taken lightly. So much interest has been aroused in these stories of Bigfoot that at least three organizations have been created to seek the creature. One is the American Resources and Development Foundation, Inc., organized by Ron Olsen, one of the most respected of all Bigfoot hunters. His organization is programing all reports of sightings on a computer in efforts to pinpoint the best possible places to continue the search.

Another is the International Wildlife Conservation Society. This group is based in Washington, D.C. At the head of it is an explorer with experience searching the Himalayas for Bigfoot's cousin, the Abominable Snowman. Even Washington socialites have helped finance the group.

Roger Patterson has also set up the Northwest Research Association. With these groups, plus uncounted individual amateur monster hunters loose in the woods, the chances seem better than ever that Bigfoot will soon slip up, be captured, measured, photographed, and verified.

Some people have admitted they plan to shoot the first Bigfoot they find, thereby ending speculation. But most hope only to take one of the furry beasts captive long enough to study him. With this in mind, expeditions go afield equipped with dart guns carrying drugs to put Bigfoot to sleep.

Patterson has mapped out a complete course of action. On that memorable day when Bigfoot is eventually tracked to earth, the procedure will include the following steps. Small groups of specialists will be scouring the mountain country for fresh evidence. "When a specimen is obtained," Patterson explains, "all personnel and equipment will be concentrated on it." Even after the effects of the drug-carrying dart wear off, Bigfoot will be kept under full sedation. (This seems safest.) All field forces will be rushed to the scene. A call will go out for a helicopter. Blood samples, bone marrow, body fluids, all will be collected and labeled. Plastic casts will be made of teeth, jaws, hands, feet, external genitalia.

Meanwhile cameras will click and whine, tape recorders will run continuously, and a stenographer will record written observations. Security measures will go into effect at once. One reason will be to protect the researchers against attack by other Bigfeet. There will also, as Patterson explains, be the need to protect the field group against ". . . interference by everybody, including the press."

Patterson welcomes new members to his association, which can be reached at P. O. Box 1101, Yakima, Washington. For their dues, members receive a certificate plus a colored photograph of Bigfoot. This is enough to make adventure-minded people everywhere feel a little closer to the monsters.

One of the most recent centers of Bigfoot activity is around the county seat town of The Dalles, Oregon. According to the sheriff's office in The Dalles, five people testified they saw the creature in the neighborhood June 2, 1971, a one-day record. A month later there was an additional sighting near the same location. Visitors flocked to town. But there were no more observations reported during the summer.

Bigfoot will almost certainly appear again. No one knows where. People all the way over into Montana and Wyoming, and other states as well, talk of the Bigfoot. Many would not be at all surprised to find these shaggy giants living in their mountains too. Doubters sometimes suggest that anyone with a mountain and a forest can have his own Sasquatch.

One thing is certain, if Bigfoot is really out there in the hills, his name belongs on the government's official list of rare and endangered species. Whatever his fortunes might have been in the past, his numbers have dwindled to a precious few.

All who seek to kill a Bigfoot should reconsider. He appears, after all, to be a harmless monster.

This is the firm belief in Skamania County, Washington. County commissioners there recently passed a law making anyone who kills a Bigfoot or Sasquatch subject to a fine of one thousand dollars and five years in jail.

To man and Bigfoot alike, this is a refreshing development. We live in an age when hundreds of wild species are becoming rare and approaching extinction. Only after the passenger pigeons were already gone did we pass laws to save them. The bison nearly became extinct for the same reason. But here is a case where we pass a law to save a wild creature even before it is found—and a monster at that.

If you should see a Bigfoot, perhaps you should tell him about that. It might help convince him that men are not such monsters after all.

13

HIDING PLACES FOR STRANGE CREATURES

THESE ARE DIFFICULT DAYS for monsters. People are almost everywhere, and people never let a monster rest.

The person who catches a fleeting glimpse of a monster spreads his story like the wind. From then on, people watch every pile of rocks, patch of brush, or hole in the hillside. Under these circumstances what chance does a monster have to find privacy? This may be why so many monsters come out only at night.

Some months ago a monster reported in the vicinity of Fort Lauderdale, Florida, made a mistake. It is said to have attacked a human. Florida, of course, has its share of monsters, but this one was something entirely new. It appeared one dark night at a drive-in movie.

A young man attending the movie wandered away from

his car. Something came up and belted him a good one, and he was knocked out colder than a popsicle. When he recovered, he found himself staring into the fur-covered face of a giant creature unlike anything he had ever seen before. Said the victim, rubbing his jaw, "I know that what I saw was no human."

The story might have died there except that other people began reporting the monster also. Four students saw it out in the Everglades in broad daylight. They reported that it had a strong body odor. Others had observed the same suffocating odors from the animal, and it became known as the "skunk ape."

The skunk ape sometimes visits trailer courts where it feeds from garbage cans. Most who see it describe it as bigger than a man, heavy bodied, and covered with brownish fur splotched with gray. Sometimes it brings along a baby skunk ape. Big hunts have been organized to run this monster to earth. So far the people around Fort Lauderdale have failed to corner the skunk ape.

People often find it difficult to believe that a creature not known to man really lives. We have a tendency to think that unless one of us has seen it, photographed it, or collected it, there is no chance it can be out there at all. But it is to people with open minds that the secrets of science are revealed.

Such searches continue, and perhaps they always will. The wild world is rich in mysterious unsolved puzzles. Around the next rock, over the next mountain peak, may lie an answer to a legend that would not die. Who can say for certain that we have answered all the questions, and that there are no mysterious creatures to find and identify?

Anyone who hopes to see a monster must beware of substitutes. There are among us people who practice monster fakery. This shameless activity takes many forms. Some years ago, in the hills of southern Ohio, there was a report of a giant snake loose in the hills. It was said to eat sheep and dogs and be a threat to even larger animals, people included.

Then, when the whole thing seemed to be quieting down, one practical joker brought it to life again. One of his friends owned an eight-foot-long boa constrictor. The snake died and the body was acquired by the monster faker. He put it into the trunk of his car and headed for the hills.

There, hidden by the night, he stretched the snake across a country road. He ran his car over it a few times, then fled the scene of his act and waited to see what happened. Three months later, seventy-five miles from the scene, he heard about giant snakes being discovered in the neighborhood where he left the corpse. "They found a whole cave full of them," he was told, "and the littlest one was eleven feet long."

Still other monster fakers fashion monster feet out of whatever materials are available. Using these phony feet, they leave a trail of giant tracks in snow and mud.

Such fakes are easily detected, however. The person responsible wants attention or he would not create a monster story in the first place. He cannot long resist the temptation to claim credit for his cleverness. The more such tracks there are, the quicker they can be identified as fake by a skilled outdoorsman. One joker only bothered to make a right foot. With it he laid a trail of tracks in the fresh snow outside his home town. People were worried until someone explained that even a monster would not go hopping around on one foot.

Serious monster hunters take such jokes in stride. They continue to explore the wild corners of the earth in search of truth. Such searches have broadened our knowledge, and revealed the presence of giant squid, Komodo dragons, and other monsters with which we share the world. What about Bigfoot, the Loch Ness monster, and a host of others? Tomorrow or the next day may bring exciting new clues concerning these as well as monsters we have not yet heard about. The great monster search will go on.

GEORGE LAYCOCK has written more than a dozen books on natural history and conservation. He has also written several hundred articles for many national magazines, including *Field and Stream*, *Sports Illustrated*, *Audubon*, *Better Homes and Gardens*, and *Boys' Life*. When he writes of animals and the outdoors, he deals with subjects of lifelong interest. He is a native of Ohio and holds a degree in wildlife management from The Ohio State University. He has traveled and camped widely, gathering information and making pictures for his articles and books.